## Praise for *Plan To Take On the World!*

"Love and compassion are necessities, not luxuries. Without them, humanity cannot survive. Within PTTOW! I had the opportunity to meet many leaders who had come together to reflect on how to live meaningful lives in service of humanity. Their commitment served as a reminder that we all share this beautiful planet Earth and therefore must learn to live together in harmony and peace."

—His Holiness the 14th Dalai Lama

"Roman Tsunder's *Plan To Take On the World!* is full of incredible stories from changemakers who have made the impossible happen. Every anecdote will have you asking yourself, 'How can I make more of an impact?' Reading this will make you feel inspired to reimagine your own life."

—Katie Couric, Journalist and Bestselling Author

"Roman Tsunder's *Plan To Take On the World!* brings the same unique energy that sets his PTTOW! apart. As someone who has innovated my entire career, I appreciate that Roman creates an environment to embrace who you are and dare to dream big and bold."

—Paris Hilton, Founder and CEO, 11:11 Media

"In *Plan To Take On the World!*, Roman Tsunder brings the stories of icons and leaders alive by sharing their strength, courage, and triumph over difficulties to do what's never been done before. With each story and accompanying lesson, Roman inspires us to transform. No matter where we come from or who harmed us, we all have the potential to change the world. *Plan To Take On the World!* is an essential read for aspiring changemakers and leaders everywhere."

—Van Jones, CNN Host and Bestselling Author

"My friend Terry Hardy and cofounder Roman Tsunder created PTTOW! to fill a void within the business community that had become deaf to the voice of the youth in the world. Roman was able to take that idea and turn it into a cultural event and network like no other. I'm proud to have been part of the early-stage idea and played a small part in shaping what it has become today. I am so stoked that Roman is sharing what he has learned with an even larger audience through this amazing book!"

—Kelly Slater, 11-time World Surf League Champion

"PTTOW! is a unique community where I've made great connections with action-oriented leaders from around the world. Roman has a unique ability to gather like-minded people who share the mission to empower youth. Their stories and passion are inspiring, and also a catalyst to depart PTTOW! with the intent to do positive things in the world."

—will.i.am, Artist and Entrepreneur

"*Plan To Take On the World!* captures the very essence of PTTOW!—a powerful reminder that when passion meets purpose, extraordinary things become possible. Roman Tsunder has built more than a community; he has sparked a global movement that inspires leaders to look inward, act boldly, and create meaningful impact in the world."

—Raja Rajamannar, Chief Marketing and Communications Officer, Mastercard

"*Plan To Take On the World!* is both a reflection and a rallying cry. Roman Tsunder shows a new generation of leaders that clarity of purpose, combined with bold action, can truly change the world."

—Jon Halvorson, Chief Digital & Marketing Officer, Kenvue

"This book is a testament to what happens when one person's vision creates space for a thousand more to flourish. Roman Tsunder carries with him not just a wealth of knowledge but an uncanny ability to connect threads that others don't even see yet. He possesses the rare gift of being able to inspire more love, deeper collaboration, and the kind of bold leaps forward that define an era."

—Nick Drake, Vice President, Global Marketing, Google

"*Plan To Take On the World!* pushes me to think that much bigger and be that much bolder about what meaningful purpose and business success can be. Putting this powerful road map in the hands of bright young minds, seasoned leaders, and everyone who is ready to chart their own fearless path means we're going to take on the world—together."

—Kory Marchisotto, President, e.l.f. Brands

# PLAN TO TAKE ON THE WORLD!

# PLAN TO TAKE ON THE WORLD!

## Spark Passion, Find Your Purpose, and Achieve the Impossible

Roman Tsunder

MATT HOLT

Matt Holt Books
An Imprint of BenBella Books, Inc.
Dallas, TX

Matt Holt is an imprint of BenBella Books, Inc.
8080 N. Central Expressway
Suite 1700
Dallas, TX 75206
benbellabooks.com
Send feedback to feedback@benbellabooks.com



Printed in the United States of America
10 9 8 7 6 5 4 3 2 1

Library of Congress Control Number: 2026021899
ISBN 9781637747247 (hardcover)
ISBN 9781637749890 (electronic)

Editing by Gregory Newton Brown
Copyediting by James Fraleigh
Proofreading by Martha Gallant and Marissa Wold Uhrina
Text design and composition by PerfecType, Nashville, TN
Cover design by Morgan Carr
Cover image © Adobe Stock / cheremuha
Printed by Lake Book Manufacturing

*To everyone who ever stood at the edge of possibility and leapt anyway—
especially my mentors and PTTOW! family, who remind me
daily what it means to dream of achieving the impossible.*

# CONTENTS

# BEFORE WE BEGIN

## I Have One Question: *Are You Ready to Do the Impossible?*

Five, four, three, two, one . . . *poof.*

All eyes in the crowd were stunned by what they were seeing. We were about to launch a human being from a cannon.

"What?!"

"Are you kidding me?!"

"Is that really . . . a . . . ?"

"Wow!"

I scanned the people on the lawn—three hundred extraordinary PTTOW! members, business leaders, icons, and masters of their craft—all gathered beside these Southern California hills under a perfect blue sky. It was the culmination of 10 years of hard work . . . and a little bit of luck. And now, for this one moment in time, they stood there together—mesmerized, mouths open in awe.

For this stunt, we'd returned to the resort venue where we'd always held events. Despite some legitimate reservations on the part of the hotel's general manager, I somehow managed to convince them everything we had been secretly planning would go off without a hitch—I wouldn't do anything to put any lives in danger. Now, there

I was, watching everyone (including the hotel GM) hold their collective breath, while the seemingly impossible was about to happen. There was no stopping the show now.

We'd offered everything you could imagine for our PTTOW! members that weekend: Wim Hof, "The Iceman," demonstrating ice baths; Kai Lenny, one of the world's greatest surfers, giving lessons; bestselling author and mind architect Dr. Joe Dispenza leading participants in manifestation meditations. We had legendary journalist Katie Couric talking about gun reform, Navy SEALs running through training exercises, members volunteering with the Boys & Girls Club of America, and so much more.

Even with all that swirling around, I was still giddy with anticipation—like my younger self at a favorite show or concert. Yet no one gathered there, not even the hotel staff, had any idea what else was about to happen. I couldn't wait to see everyone's faces.

Amid the chaos, I knew my favorite part of the show—as I like to call our summits—was about to begin, and I was trying to keep it together. About two-thirds of the way through lunch, on a perfect, sunny Southern California day just off the beach, the countdown began—15, 14, 13 . . .

The WOW portion was about to begin. *Step right up, ladies and gentlemen . . .*

It was three years in the making. Our team had scoured the country looking for someone who could pull this feat off—and someone who had the equipment for it. Only two people in the US could do it, both based on the East Coast. After convincing one of them to drive his giant, tarp-covered contraption across the country, he was finally here and about to soar.

A big poof of smoke burst from the cannon . . .

The moment froze in time. I looked at all of my friends and peers, all the members of PTTOW!—necks flung back, their eyes fixed on the sky. I could barely tear my eyes away from them but did so long enough to look up and see David "The Bullet" Smith, the human cannonball, soar over us—nearly two hundred feet through the air before landing in a giant net on the far side of the lawn.

Why would someone do such a thing? Why would anyone put themselves in a cannon and launch into the sky?

Why not?

Why not do the impossible?

Why not defy the limitations of gravity, time, and space?

If we can dream it, we can do it. That's why we created PTTOW! That's why everyone was gathered that year, at the 2019 summit we had aptly themed "Higher Calling"—to remind ourselves of the impossible.

*Why not fly?*

*Human Cannonball David "The Bullet" Smith launching over PTTOW! members at the 2019 "Higher Calling" Summit (Photo by Casey Tang)*

# INTRODUCTION

## *Your Permission Slip to Take On the World*

I've always chased WOW moments.

My desire to wow and inspire goes back as far as I can recall. As a kid, I remember walking through a tunnel to the nosebleed seats in Anaheim Stadium and seeing the enormous field and spectacle of lights for the first time. Wow. Everything stopped for me. It all went white. It happened again at 14, at my first concert at Irvine Meadows—Michael Jackson on his *Bad* world tour. I didn't know it then, but the awe and wonder I felt set me on a journey I wasn't yet aware of. My subconscious wanted to escape—to be a performer or a ringleader. I felt a deep-seated desire to be part of the show, part of the awe and wonder. It's like my soul knew what it wanted before I did.

But my conscious mind? It lived in the world of roles and expectations. Everyone around me wanted to be doctors, lawyers, bankers. Nobody came to school on career day as a performer or ringmaster.

Still, that dream of being part of the "show" persisted. And over time, it revealed itself in the form of passions, interests—and eventually, PTTOW! A dream that began unconsciously took shape consciously when I cofounded PTTOW! in 2009 with Terry Hardy (manager to skateboarder Tony Hawk and surfer Kelly Slater) and independent filmmaker Jim Sullos.

Ten years later, in April 2019, I was standing on the lawn of the beautiful Monarch Beach Hotel in Laguna Beach, awaiting the human cannonball shoot across the lawn, surrounded by people having lunch after three days of keynotes, think tanks, activities, meet-ups, town halls, and once-in-a-lifetime experiences. Members included CEOs, chief marketing officers (CMOs), creatives, and culture shapers from companies like MTV, iHeart, The North Face, TOMS, Quiksilver, LVMH, Anheuser-Busch, Universal Music Group, Hilton, Meta, Cirque du Soleil, Chase, Airbnb, Uber, Xbox, and T-Mobile. They all had one thing in common: They had shaped global culture.

From the beginning, PTTOW! was meant to operate outside the status quo. We created a platform that gives, spreads, and multiplies positive messages. What I've seen over the years has changed me. At every event, every curated conversation, every summit, we ask ourselves and our members, Why am I here? What's my purpose? How big can I dream? What's my impact? How can I grow our brand?

I asked those questions of myself in 2009. I still do.

Kelly Slater, Terry's client, suggested the name PTTOW!—inspired by the cartoon *Pinky and the Brain*. They had a *Plan To Take Over the World*. We loved it. Not the term "over" part—we weren't planning on world domination. But what if everyone could answer the question, *What's your **P**lan **T**o **T**ake **O**n the **W**orld*?

With that, PTTOW! was born.

We gave this community a name that sounds like a comic book—PTTOW!—because we wanted it to feel larger than life, like a group of modern-day Avengers. Each of our annual programs explores a theme: Higher Calling, Hero's Journey, Chasing True North, Metamorphosis, Phoenix Rising, and Kintsugi. They're more than themes—they're invitations. To reflect. To transform. To be inspired. To grow. To turn failures into gold.

We wanted to give leaders the space to consider their journey—and a megaphone via this platform to share it. We wanted to provide a space where they could connect with their peers, learn from today's greatest minds, and springboard their companies to greater success.

We wanted to inspire WOW moments, because when we're inspired, we can defy reality. We can dream big and do the NBDB—the Never Been Done Before.

And speaking of the impossible: the idea that I, Roman Tsunder, would have cofounded PTTOW! with Terry Hardy and Jim Sullos seemed impossible in 2009.

It wasn't even meant to be a business. It was just a passion project.

Back then, I was also the founder and president of Access 360 Media, which had built one of the largest out-of-home media networks in America—kind of like MTV meets FashionTV while you shop—an idea I originally dreamed up after seeing the movie *Minority Report* with Tom Cruise. I was passionate about youth culture, which comprised nearly 60% of the world's population, and I realized there was no Davos or Allen & Company retreat or TED for the type of leader whose company's lifeblood and future were in the hands of young people. All the existing organizations served the establishment. We wanted to serve the innovators, the rule breakers, those shaping tomorrow's culture.

Yet events like these were hard to come by. I had attended so many sessions, conferences, and trade shows. But they were all so boring and uninspiring. I realized I'd been going to the wrong places with the wrong people and having the wrong conversations. Speakers were there just to feed their egos. The audience was just waiting in line to give them their business card or pitch something. The events were often one and done. Lasting relationships were never formed. And they usually happened in bland conference rooms that felt right out of an episode of *The Office*.

Then I thought: *What if?*

*What if* the audience was more influential than the speakers on stage?

*What if* each person represented a different industry and expertise?

*What if* we created an IMAX experience to WOW and share groundbreaking projects and stories?

*What if* we created a year-round, living, breathing community that members could be part of versus just going to?

*What if* we created a community that could help change the world, one person and topic at a time?

Then I thought*: If not me*, then who?

*If not now*, then when?

So I started from zero.

The energy was building, and I knew if this was going to happen, it would have to come through me.

I started with the idea of bringing 20 leaders from different industries together. Bob McKnight, the CEO of Quiksilver, was one of the first people to join, representing action sports—mostly I think because the event was only 20 minutes away from his office. Terry Hardy, my cofounder, was (and still is) Kelly Slater's manager, and he was the face of Quiksilver at the time.

I'd always been a huge fan of youth culture—especially MTV, which I grew up on. MTV ushered in a generation of young Gen Xers and Millennials, who then became Facebook, Snapchat, and TikTok users. Watching this progression and watching PTTOW! grow (Bob Pittman and Tom Freston, the heads of MTV, and Sir Lucian Grainge, CEO of Universal Music Group, had even become a part of our community) got me thinking.

Who are all the leaders who are influencing young people right now in every industry?

Why not get 20 of *them* together in a room?

Soon we had Activision and YouTube leaders sign on. Then the CMO of Hewlett-Packard. Then the head of branding for Procter & Gamble.

People sometimes ask me how I got these leaders into one room together. I did it by talking passionately to each leader, one at a time, and finding the pressing problem they needed to solve. I've had thousands of conversations over the past 15 years with leaders from all over the world.

As exciting as it was to get 20 responses, I had emailed and invited hundreds of leaders. But those 20 were the ones who understood the mission. They bought into my passion that the future of their companies' success was in the hands of young people, but that there was NOWHERE for them to go to learn from each other and collaborate together other than this group we were creating, PTTOW!

Just two years later while on vacation with a few friends to clear my mind after a difficult year, I had another "aha!" moment:

What if PTTOW! could be an actual business itself?

Everyone told me it was a bad idea. They said there was no business model. People wouldn't show up. It couldn't work. It had no industry focus, as trade shows for tech, consumer goods, sports, and gaming did. Besides, no one had ever put leaders from disparate industries into rooms together.

Their criticism didn't make any sense to me. How could people disrupt their industries, learn from each other, and find partners if they were all from the same space?

Of course, I understood it from the naysayers' point of view. An idea like PTTOW! didn't check any of the boxes that entrepreneurs typically look for—total addressable market, business model, ease of explanation, scalability, and so forth. But it checked a box that I had never thought of before: *I loved it and was clearly passionate about it.*

So I said to myself: *What if I forget about how big the addressable market is? What if I do this because I am passionate about it and see where this leads?*

This idea led to an organization that, like Davos, the Aspen Ideas Festival, or TED, convenes some of the most influential, culture-shaping minds and brands in the world—more than three hundred corporate members, ranging from Netflix to Google, Coca-Cola to Spotify, Procter & Gamble to Mastercard. These are the companies shaping our world and redefining how we connect, create, and contribute. Alongside them are our Icon members—leaders whose contributions to their chosen fields have not only globally impacted culture but have transcended the boundaries of their industries to redefine the very scope of their professions. Over the years, the Icon ranks have grown into an extraordinary constellation of leaders—including His Holiness the Dalai Lama, Quincy Jones, Kelly Slater, and Halle Berry—whose collective impact has touched billions. But more important than their names is the spirit they bring: creativity, generosity, and the courage to take on the world.

Our decade-long partnership with the Nelson Mandela Foundation and Africa Rising Foundation gave us the great gift of being able to shine a spotlight on leaders and organizations who were carrying on the legacy of President Mandela through their own efforts. PTTOW!'s Nelson Mandela Changemaker Award gave us a powerful vehicle to celebrate and accelerate the efforts of these extraordinary leaders and communities who are creating real, tangible change around the globe.

Today, PTTOW! is a living, breathing year-round community. Our platform spans nearly 20 touchpoints a year, from verticals like PTTOW! Sports and PTTOW! Entertainment, to intimate salons that spark collaborations you won't find anywhere else. We've hosted our summits at world-class destinations such as the Terranea Resort in Rancho Palos Verdes, the Waldorf Astoria Monarch Beach, and Montage Deer Valley, and created experiences at some of the world's biggest stages—from Cannes Lions in France, to the Super Bowl, to the Hamptons, and beyond. With the launch of PTTOW! Europe, our reach is expanding globally. To date, we've catalyzed more than two hundred projects and partnerships between member brands—initiatives we've originated, accelerated, or pushed over the finish line. These aren't ordinary projects; they are sparks that ignite change: a campaign that redefined how a generation sees gun safety, partnerships that transform how brands engage in music and sports, and collaborations that unlock new market opportunities.

The true measure of PTTOW! isn't just in the number of partnerships. It's in the way it has become a trusted force where leaders and brands come to learn, step out of competition and into connection and collaboration, and shape culture with an impact that ripples across industries and communities worldwide.

Over the past 15 years, I've had a front-row seat to some of the most influential minds on the planet—visionaries in business, entertainment, sports, activism, and tech. I've been in the rooms where the real conversations happen. And after thousands of honest, raw, and sometimes messy moments with these leaders, one thing is clear: People who truly move the world aren't just chasing goals—they're chasing something deeper. They're driven by purpose. They're obsessed. Not with money, titles, or status—but with doing something meaningful. And that healthy obsession—paired with humility, resilience, and a relentless belief in the impossible—is what sets them apart.

But I didn't just witness this. I lived it. I've spent 25 years building companies, chasing big dreams, and—just as important—doing the inner work it takes to truly lead. The most powerful growth didn't happen on stages or spreadsheets. It happened in the quiet moments. The breakdowns. The breakthroughs. The years of unlearning, healing, and getting real with myself. That's why at the end of each chapter, you'll find exercises—not because I think you need to be fixed, but because I know how powerful it is when you finally ask yourself the right questions. For me, it wasn't until I understood *who I was* and *why I was* that I could finally see what I truly wanted. And that changed everything. PTTOW! was off and running.

Since then, I've welcomed so many of my heroes to our community and created moments we'll remember forever.

And every time I do, I'm reminded: This isn't about me. It's about what we can share and build—together.

As a kid born in communist Russia who came to the US as an immigrant, I never imagined this life.

And that's why I'm writing this book.

I wrote this book for people seeking greatness.

I wrote this book because I didn't have it when I was just starting out.

I wrote it for you: the dreamers, the doers, the big thinkers, future legends, icons, heroes of their own life story, the entrepreneurs, the brand leaders, the young professionals just starting out, the mid-career professionals looking to level up or even make a greater impact, the future changemakers—so you'd have the insight, information, and inspiration for your own plan that I didn't when I started out.

I wrote this so you could

*live your wildest and most impossible dreams,*
*dare to do the NBDB and create a Plan To Take On the World, and*

*leave the comforts of your life as you know it and venture to uncharted territory.*

This book is for those who are willing to Plan To Take On the World!

If you picked up this book, it's no accident. You're here for a reason. So, What Is Your Plan To Take On the World?

I ask because I want to bring a sense of possibility to you.

PTTOW! may be one of the world's most exclusive communities, but this book is for everyone! I want to use the messages, ideas, and learning from 15 years of experiences with creators, entrepreneurs, leaders, and visionaries to help you answer these questions:

What if success isn't what we've been taught?

What if your idea of success needs to be rewritten?

What if you could build your own plan—to take on the world?

Consider this book your permission slip.

Think of *Plan To Take On the World!* as a simple guide to help you awaken to your purpose, spark your passion, and make your most impossible dreams come true. This isn't a prescriptive, "how-to" book. This is simply a guide. Take what you love and leave the rest behind. Whatever speaks to you, inspires you, and motivates you to begin, great. My purpose is to share my own story—including the improbable origin of PTTOW!—along with the stories of many of our members who dared to do the NBDB, so you can begin to rewrite your own story.

You can become the hero of your life. And as you begin this journey, I reiterate: I want to be your partner or guide, not your instructor.

You'll learn the same lessons that some of the most influential people in the world have employed to launch WOW moment after WOW moment.

Too often, we find ourselves driving forward but looking at our life through the rearview mirror, simply living our future lives the way we lived our past. But what if we looked through a new window onto an exciting and inspiring new superhighway instead? I simply want to be your guide, so you can connect with your deeper self, your higher self, and create the life of your dreams—one that will be legendary.

As you read, listen to your body. Ask yourself what resonates. Our soul—our gut, our intuition—already knows what's true for us. When something feels "right," we feel it in our body: an openness, a lightness, a spark. When it's not right, we often feel contraction, resistance, and tightness. Pay attention to that. Let your body and your soul guide you.

Fifteen years ago, when we started PTTOW!, I wished we had a book like this. We were chasing something impossible. And in doing that, we had to reframe what success meant.

From the age of six, the world begins to define success for us—our parents, teachers, friends. They mean well. They tell us to go after the safe and stable: the house, the job title, the big bank account. I call those "first mountain" goals.

But too often, we reach the top and realize we feel empty inside. We only look successful on the outside. I want to invite you to redefine success as something deeper—where joy and fulfillment come not from material things, but from finding your purpose. That fire inside you. The gifts only you can bring.

This book is about fanning the flames of the desires already burning within you. My only goal is to help you remember who you are, what makes you come alive, and what your soul came here to do. You can still have the house, the title, the bank account—you can have it all. But now, you'll be getting it your way. Aligned with who you really are.

## OVERVIEW OF THE PTTOW! JOURNEY

So what can you expect from *Plan To Take On the World*?

We'll start with part 1: "Own Your Story." Every great story has a hero, and you are that hero. In chapter 1, you'll discover your origin story, the one that reveals what truly drives you. In chapter 2, you'll learn how to let love be your compass, not fear, and how Bert Jacobs, cofounder of Life Is Good, built not just a business but a lifestyle rooted in positivity, gratitude, and love. You'll also learn how surfing legend Kelly Slater faced his fears and rode the wave to greatness. In chapter 3, you'll learn how to fan the flames and understand the interplay of your passion and purpose, learning from music legend and icon Quincy Jones. In chapter 4, you'll identify and nurture your natural talents, just as Olympic gold-medalist snowboarder Shaun White did. In chapter 5, you'll break out of your routine and intentionally place yourself in new environments that spark fresh ideas, new perspectives, and unexpected inspiration. In chapter 6, you'll do the deeper inner work—facing the parts of yourself you've avoided—so you can unlock a more authentic, whole version of who you are. And in chapter 7, you'll learn how to align your body and mind. Through stories and exercises, you'll begin to shape a vision for your own next chapter and formulate a plan for how to get from your present self to your future self.

Part 2, "Work Your Plan," will help you focus on embodying that new version of yourself. In chapter 8, you'll learn what it takes to "go O.H.F."—or become Obsessed and put in the Hours with blackout Focus—as Quincy Jones did when working on his music, or Paris Hilton did when building her empire, or my team and I did when launching PTTOW! In chapter 9, we name the impossible goal you've been struggling to declare. You'll learn from record-breaking swimmer Diana Nyad, who did what was once thought impossible.

In chapter 10, you'll turn your purpose into practice—learning how to commit to the work that brings it to life, and how to find meaning and joy in showing up for it every day, even when it's hard. In chapter 11, you'll expand your vision—challenging what you've been told is possible and learning to pursue a path that's truly your own.

In chapter 12, you'll face and conquer your fears like skier-turned-pilot Janine Shepherd did. In chapter 13, you'll master rejection and failure, and in chapter 14, you'll finally take the leap—pro skateboarder Danny Way will lead the way! Through daily practices, you'll learn how to live with greater purpose, presence, and creativity.

By part 3, "Share Your Plan," you will have learned so much about yourself that you'll have the tools and inspiration to take your life to the next level. Now I'll share how you can take your own stories and talents out into the world. In chapter 16, you'll realize you will go further by becoming radically generous. You'll learn how from some of the most generous people I know: Daniel Flynn, the founder of social enterprise company Thankyou, and Blake Mycoskie, founder of charitable shoe seller TOMS. In chapter 17, you'll become radically accountable for all you do by following "Poker Princess" Molly Bloom's incredibly redemptive example. In chapter 18, you'll become far more vulnerable, learning that there is strength in softness, as Heather Malenshek, senior vice president and chief marketing officer for Land O'Lakes, shares with us. In chapter 19, you'll learn how to go together—because no one takes on the world alone. In chapter 20, you'll learn how to create experiences that captivate and wow—just as Raja Rajamannar, chief marketing and communications officer at Mastercard, and Mark Weinstein, chief marketing officer at Hilton, do every day with all the people they serve.

You'll reflect. You'll reimagine. You'll take on your world.

Think of this book as your launchpad. A cannon shot that will launch you into a limitless mindset—one that unlocks a new way of being. I hope it sparks previously impossible quantum leaps. I hope you ask yourself: What makes me come most alive? How can you get "everything you didn't know you wanted?" What would it take to WOW me? What would impress my six-year-old self? What makes you feel a little giddy with excitement? What is your why? These are just a few questions I hope we can explore together and answer.

Ultimately, this book is designed to take you on your journey—your impossible journey. It begins with the first step. And sometimes, that step means going forward when everyone else is standing still.

So let the countdown begin—five, four, three, two, one . . .

Let's fly!

# Part 1

# Take On the World by Owning Your Story

Clark Kent. Bruce Wayne. Wonder Woman. Peter Parker. Luke Skywalker. Cinderella. What do all of these characters have in common? Whether a superhero, demigod, space fighter, or princess, each one became a hero of their own stories. Before they became Superman, Batman, an Amazon Warrior, Spider-Man, a Jedi, or a princess, they started with an origin story. Commonly known as the Hero's Journey, this archetypal structure has been used in stories throughout the world since the dawn of storytelling itself. Though it was by no means his idea, mythology scholar Joseph Campbell recognized that all heroes follow the same narrative stages—as do most humans. We are, after all, as Campbell noted, "the heroes of our own story."

Campbell detailed 17 stages in all, divided across three simple phases: the Departure, the Initiation, and the Return. In Departure, some catalyst propels our hero on a quest; during Initiation, they face many trials on the journey; and in Return, they prevail, then return to their community to share their gifts and new wisdom.

We're all on a Hero's Journey. I know I am not alone. Over the years, I have benefited from listening to PTTOW! members share their own origin stories, incredible and harrowing life-and-death journeys, and all they have learned from their own trials and tribulations. They've made me pause and reflect on my own impossible journey—or what I call my *I-Am-Possible Journey*. My hope is that this section invites you to stop, pause, and consider your own origin story—and your own purpose. We all start somewhere, and it's that start that holds the keys to not only our superpowers but our greatest adventure. Often a story is being told that we don't see on the surface, but the universe may have its own plans. And as ever, *Plan To Take On the World!* begins with a brave first step . . .

# Chapter 1

# Understand Your Origin Story

You are the hero of your own story.

—Joseph Campbell

In 1978, I won the refugee lottery. Thanks to some well-meaning do-gooders, my family, Jewish refugees being persecuted in Odessa, Ukraine, were invited to live in the United States. After my mother convinced my reluctant father to join her, she gathered us, made her plan, and with less than $100 to her name moved us to Los Angeles.

It might as well have been like landing on the moon to five-year-old me.

My parents had no jobs lined up, no money, and didn't speak the language. All my mom knew was an aunt had come before us. My Aunt Riva and Uncle Joseph were extremely generous people and gave my mother $300 to buy an old Chevrolet. With that bounty, we were on our way to securing the first part of the American Dream—a car.

The second part was a career. My mom was no slouch: She was educated, persistent, and resourceful, and is still working to this day.

She learned the language quickly, and so did my sister Renee and I. Then she parlayed her engineering degree into a job at the audio equipment maker JBL and my father picked up carpenter jobs wherever he could find them to make ends meet.

Despite my parents' best efforts, we were all strangers in a strange land. We had no idea what we were doing. I recall we all were walking down the streets of Los Angeles and watching people eating in a restaurant gleaming with beautiful brass rails. It all looked so ornate and fancy. I clearly remember my mother saying, "We'll save up our money and come back." True to her word, we did, and we ate a feast at *Carl's Jr.* What did we know? Everything was foreign, different, and bizarre. In Russia, no one said, "How are you?" as a greeting. But in America, when someone asked my mother that, she would say, "Pull up a chair. Sit. Let me tell you." She was so innocent, still is, and yet so real. She is a force of a woman, an entrepreneur and innovator, determined to make it in this new country, and wanted the same for her children. She wasn't satisfied with the status quo. She was always looking for ways to improve our lives.

When we first arrived, we lived in an area off Fairfax Avenue that was a bit like a little Russia. It was as if we were living in a Russian bubble—everyone there still spoke Russian, ate Russian meals, and kept the Russian culture alive in the neighborhood. There was a park nearby called "lunch park" that would hand out free lunches to poorish families like us, and so we lived in the Fairfax District for a bit, enjoying the generosity and safety of the somewhat familiar neighborhood.

Once my grandparents arrived six months later, my mother was able to work full time without worrying about me and Renee. We became latchkey kids, with grandparents who checked in on us. My mom soon started an interior decorating company and moved us to Lake Forest in Orange County, securing the third part of the

American Dream—a home. My parents had visited Laguna Beach and fell in love with the ocean, since it reminded them of their home back in Odessa. Of course, we couldn't afford to actually live in Laguna Beach, but being "beach adjacent" was good enough. It was there, now far removed from the Russian culture of Fairfax and free lunches in the park, that I started to realize not only how different things in America were but how different *I was.* I wasn't running into poor Russian Jewish kids in Lake Forest.

From the outset in beautiful Orange County, I desperately wanted to fit in. I learned quickly how to adapt and do whatever all the other kids were doing, to fit in. Whether it was the clothes, the haircut, playing sports, or hanging out with friends eating lunch, I tried my best to not pull focus. For a while I simply observed, and it was from observing that I realized how I could eventually entertain and keep my audience distracted from the fact I was so "different." Instead of a "ringleader," I became the class clown.

For instance, in fifth grade, when a substitute teacher came in, I had the class tell her I was a foreign exchange student from Russia and didn't speak any English. I had another kid translate the entire class to me. I entertained the whole class that day and had a blast.

However, I was always well aware that there were the kids who weren't laughing with me, but rather at me. I still feel the sting of being made fun of for being from Russia and being called a commie. At the time, I felt pretty powerless. I never stood up for myself. Instead I tried to laugh it off or laugh with them and be in on the joke. Even though it hurt me, I never let them know it. In a way, I was building armor around me, which I would wear for a very long time. I knew what it took to be likable, charming, and get my way, even in a tough or unwilling crowd—even if it was a heavy weight to bear.

At the most basic level, our universal longing to belong is what sets us all on a quest of discovery. When we are young, we think we are off to discover the world, but we are in fact about to embark on the greatest discovery of a lifetime—who we really are and what our own deepest longings and desires are. From a young age, I was seeking not just belonging and approval, but a desire to wow, inspire, captivate, and entertain—to stand out and be seen. I see that now as an adult looking back at little Roman . . . he was trying so hard to make his friends laugh, while also trying to fit in, because deep inside he knew he wanted to be so much more than the world was seeing.

I know I am not alone. We all have a unique origin story. We all have a primal longing that sets us on our quest to follow a dream. My mother's quest began when she gathered her family and left all she knew behind her to start over and fulfill the American Dream. Mine started the day I realized I wanted more—could be more—if I could just break out from the crowd—to be Roman, and not the person stuck in a reality he didn't like.

In a way, all of this longing, this desire to be seen and accepted, made me feel like an outsider. But as all heroes discover during the course of their origin story, my superpower was born. Just as Superman didn't know his own strength until his mettle was tested as a young child, I didn't know my abilities to talk, inspire, and bring people together, until I had no choice but to use them.

---

ACTIVITY

## Understand Your Origin Story To Take On the World

I find it helpful to have a notebook or a Google Doc open when I'm reading so I can take notes and respond to any activities and reflections. You don't have to do these exercises, but to truly get the most out of this book, and to have a taste of what breakout sessions and activities at PTTOW! events are like, I recommend taking some time to respond to the prompts at the end of each chapter.

## Step 1: Free-Write Your Origin Story

What do I mean by free-write? Don't sweat the small stuff. You're not being graded. No one but you will be reading this, so just start getting things down on paper. It's okay to misspell, riff, and use poor grammar; write from your heart. The point is not to be perfect, but to be authentic and honest. My friend Jonathan Hudson first took me through this exercise, and I found it deeply impactful.

Try free-writing a letter to an imaginary person in the future about your origin story. Include the events that had a significant impact on you emotionally, and how these things affect your life now. Was there a time you felt left out? Wanted to belong? Struggled with some challenge or perceived shortcoming, failure, or life circumstance? Be as specific as possible. Continue writing until you feel you have gotten everything down on paper. Write as many pages as you need.

## Step 2: Condensation

Read through your free-write until you begin seeing the meat of your letter. Think in terms of summarizing. Circle and underline the key parts. When you feel into it completely, condense your letter into one paragraph that captures the core essence of your free-writing.

## Step 3: Essence

Finding the essence of something means finding the "feeling" of it. To do so, you may need to read over paragraphs aloud. Begin to let go of the words that are written; focus all of your attention on the feeling this paragraph invokes. When you get clear on this feeling, write *one or two words* that encapsulate it. (Words that come to mind might be: Sad. Depressed. Victim. Angry. Lonely. Longing.)

## Step 4: Look for the Opposite

Once you boil the letter down to one or two essential words that describe your origin story, concentrate on them. Really feel the word or words you wrote down. Ask yourself, if this feeling had an opposite, what would it be? As you feel the opposite, write it down. For example, if the word you ended up with was "Victim," the opposite word you're looking for wouldn't be "Victor." It would be something like "Empowered," "Creator," or "Powerful."

Congratulations, this is your new Hero Identity!

## Step 5: Create Your Own Reality

Take the word you found to be opposite and create a sentence from that word—something that you desire to be true in your life now. When you complete this sentence, expand that sentence into a paragraph. Then, do another free-write about your new Hero Identity.

## Step 6: Integration Meditation

If you've never meditated before, don't overthink it. Even a few minutes of stillness, in an age of always-on notifications and constant distractions, can rewire your brain, calm your body, and help you fully *become* your new identity. Close your eyes, focus on your breathing, and let yourself be. This meditation will integrate or bring together your new identity.

Now, imagine yourself climbing up the tallest mountain in the world. When you get to the top, see the word from your old identity BIG in the sky. Take a big red marker and cross it out while you say, "NO!" Then send it off to burn up in the sun. See it burn. Smell it burn. Feel the heat. Hear it crackle. Use all of your senses and make it real. This identity is DONE.

Now write your new word big in the sky with a different-color marker, and say, "YES!!!" Yell out to the entire planet, "THIS IS MY NEW IDENTITY!!! I AM [insert new identity here]!" And see the billions of people on the planet looking up at you and cheering, recognizing and supporting you in your new identity.

Do this until you feel it in every cell of your body. Don't stop until you've made it real!

# Chapter 2

# Let Love, Not Fear, Be Your Compass

> The choice that frees or imprisons us is the choice of love or fear. Love liberates. Fear imprisons.
>
> —Gary Zukav

While speaking at an event recently, I asked everyone there to tap into a time when they felt as though they were alive—really, truly alive. The goal was for them to imagine feeling joyful, expansive, full of hope and anticipation. I was trying to help them relive this moment so that it might illuminate their purpose. I had already explained the process for them to find their purpose, and now I was trying to help them access it.

Then someone raised their hand and said, "I feel nothing. What if I have no purpose?" He went on to claim he'd never had a moment when he felt absolute oneness, flow, joy, expansion. And he had resigned himself to the belief that he had no purpose.

I thought for a second. It was clear this person was frozen. He was so cut off from his own present emotions, he couldn't feel anything. So many of us have experienced trauma in our lives, forcing us to develop built-in response mechanisms that help us survive. In the parlance of trauma-informed therapy, which I have learned from training at the Stanford Compassion Institute, Dr. Joe Dispenza's retreats, Transcendental Meditation, somatic healing work, and 25 years of therapy, we respond to trauma with flight, fight, freeze, or fawn modes.

Most of us are familiar with flight or fight. But few of us realize that we also freeze or fawn when traumatized too. Freezing simply means the cessation of inner feelings—good or bad. We freeze in order to survive extremely painful physical or emotional traumas. Some of us also learn to "fawn"—that is, look and act nonthreatening—as a means of subjection. We slump our shoulders, play it small, become soft spoken and overly pleasing, and even take on a subservient, even admiring role with the people abusing or mistreating us—all in an effort to survive.

Many of us are unaware we are even acting out of trauma responses—that is to say, fear. We may be so used to cutting and running or freezing and fawning the moment times get tough, we may think it's part of our personality—"This is just who I am!" Some of us can become so reactive and defensive, we may spend our days with our guard up, always looking for a fight, unaware we've adopted this behavior to protect ourselves from perceived outside threats.

The problem is, of course, the traumatic event has long been over—but it lives inside us. And until we identify it, feel it, and release it, we'll continue to react in the same old ways—long after the survival mechanism no longer serves us.

This was clearly the case for the man who claimed he had no purpose. He was afraid of something—what, I didn't know. I am sure even he didn't know. All I did know was he felt frozen—paralyzed in doubt. At some point in this young man's life he "froze" to survive. Subconsciously, he must have felt it was better not to feel anything in order to cope with life and get through the day. But, as they say, "what helps you survive doesn't help you thrive." If he wanted to access his purpose, he would have to first access his emotions and begin to feel.

So I pushed him: "Let me ask you another question. Was there a time from the age of six years old that you felt some sort of ember-like excitement about something in your life?" All I was looking for was an ember—not the whole fire of feeling. I understood that might be tough for him.

And not surprisingly, he answered, "Yeah, I remember that there was an excitement at that age."

"Okay," I said, "I want you to think about that. Our finding our purpose is a little bit like finding a pilot light, right? The work is now to turn that pilot light into a wild flame, and we do that by fanning the flames. Where there is an ember, there is where the work needs to be. Your job now is to give more energy and focus to that ember."

What this exchange made me realize is that so many of us shut down our joy, excitement, and enthusiasm for the things we enjoy in order to survive. This man, like so many, had put up so much armor around himself and his heart, he couldn't feel. It wasn't his fault, whatever had happened to him, but the opportunity for him is to find that ember of glow and fan those flames.

You have to identify that feeling and lean into the flame, igniting it and giving it oxygen, blowing on it, paying attention to it, adding sticks, then adding fuel. You have to keep doing it.

That's where you get to the next level, the expansion, the joy, because you can't feel it right now.

The reality is, love feels like coming to ourselves. We know at a cellular level what feels good—expansive, joyful, happy, appreciative, inspired.

We also know what we fear—our body feels tight, contracted, protective, tense. What are you doing when you feel like you have to have your guard up? That is *not* what you should be doing. That is a sign your body is calling out to you to stop. By contrast, what are you doing when you feel excited? Happy? Joyful? Relaxed? Light?

It comes down to two feelings—love and fear.

All positive emotions lead you toward love, oneness, and your alignment with your purpose.

All negative emotions—fear, envy, resentment, anger—illuminate what you are resisting.

This duality of love and fear is constantly at work. Knowing how to recognize and identify these feelings is the key to understanding your purpose, and following the feelings is key to living your purpose.

When I feel love, abundance, and gratitude, I feel an expansion in my chest. It's an open feeling—a feeling of possibility. I want to spread my arms out wide as if to hug someone.

Fear feels like wanting to fight, run, freeze, control, ball up your fists, contract. You often feel it in the belly or solar plexus first, just below your diaphragm.

There is, however, an exception to this—and it takes some work and getting comfortable identifying your feelings. Sometimes, when we get excited to do something, we have a momentary feeling of panic, fear, and worry that things may not work out or we'll get hurt or fail. Our body seizes up. Even though we know our purpose, our life, our joy—our mind—gets the better of us.

We have all been there—in the death spiral of thinking about the past, old mistakes, or what others may have said about us. We get in our own head and we let those thoughts determine our feelings. Before long we're talking ourselves out of our own joy. It's not an accident. Our thoughts can change how we feel. Just by ruminating on the past we can begin to feel anxious or worry about the future, and all the worst-case scenarios can put us into a panic.

Conversely, slowing our thoughts and replacing them with feelings of appreciation, or recalling a happier time or part of the day, can begin to calm us. Even distraction can change our moods. It can also become magnetic—the energy we put out will attract similar energy.

No one knows this better than Bert Jacobs—he and his brother JJ founded the Life is Good™ company. He is a longtime PTTOW! member and has spoken at several of our summits. Bert shared how optimism is a practice. It changed his and his brother's lives—and led them to form America's original positive lifestyle brand.

When Bert and JJ were kids, their family was not making ends meet financially. But their mother's powerful optimism got them through difficult times. Despite raising them in a household with an often-depressed husband who expressed his struggles through anger, their mother created a transformative ritual at the dinner table. Every night she asked each of her six children to "tell me something good that happened today." This simple practice taught the brothers that their disposition was powerful—and could be magnetic. While there was plenty of dysfunction in the home, taking the time to celebrate good things changed the energy and made them feel resilient.

Over time, Bert and JJ realized that by acknowledging negative aspects of their lives but focusing on the positive aspects of their day could literally change the energy in their environment too. This foundational lesson became the cornerstone of their business philosophy—that wherever you put your energy and focus, that is the energy that will grow. Bert and his brother found that optimists naturally attract other optimists, and they built a $250 million business on this idea. It's the same principle I've seen again and again: The story you choose to tell yourself can either limit you or liberate you.

During our summit, Bert shared how he read an article one day about a young girl, Lindsay Beggett, who wore a Life is Good hat while battling terminal cancer. When the reporter asked her if she understood what "terminal" meant, she said she did. Then the reporter incredulously asked if she still wanted to wear a hat that says "Life is Good."

"Of course," she said. She then went on to explain that her illness taught her not to take life for granted. That every day was a gift.

When Bert read this, he was stunned. That single answer captured the very heartbeat of the brand—and reminded us all that optimism isn't naive, it's defiant. It's choosing courage in the face of fear. And Lindsay also made him realize that having a positive outlook provides access to courage and gratitude. It's a superpower and can transform anyone—even those facing death.

At the end of his talk, Bert surprised everyone with a video of Lindsay. That same girl who was given a year to live—somehow survived! At 17 years old she reunited with Bert and talked about the power of her attitude, gratitude, optimism, and the belief that Life is Good—and how it changed her.

It changed all of us.

My point is, no matter how hard life is, there is always hope. There is always so much to be grateful for and so much to love. All suffering is temporary. Don't confuse yourself. Don't psych yourself out. The key is, once you have tapped into the expansive feeling of your purpose, you have to ride the wave. And if you can root that purpose in optimism—like Bert, like Lindsay, like so many of our members—you don't just ride the wave. You can shift the entire current of what's possible.

Kelly Slater, the world's greatest surfer and PTTOW! Icon, knows his purpose. He knows when he is in flow. Right as he's about to drop into a wave, does fear hold him back? No. He has said on several occasions that within the ocean there are any number of dangers—he could fall off his board and be pulled under, he could be attacked by a shark, he could be thrown into rocks and die as some of his peers have. There are innumerable dangers.

Yet if he allowed thoughts of these dangers or the discomfort of facing his fears to dominate him, he would be seized by them. He wouldn't be able to tap into his flow. The two feelings can't exist together. If he were to let fear take a vice grip on him, he wouldn't be able to feel the waves churn beneath him or flow through him—he would wipe out. Instead, he reframes fear and uses it to his advantage. Rather than telling himself he's afraid, he tells himself he's excited. The shift keeps him alert, alive, and open. He knows he's about to do something no one has done before when he feels this fear coming on. He has learned to distinguish it—and to harness it.

This is a key reframe we can all use. If you find yourself stepping into an important meeting with a natural instinct of fear, a simple shift can make a difference. Simply pause, recognize you are in fight or flight, and then reframe the meeting in your mind about how excited the potential of the meeting has made you. (And by the way, you will enjoy the meeting and energy that much more.) Fear becomes fuel.

Kelly's story shows us that purpose isn't about eliminating fear; it's about transforming it. He turns fear into energy, and that energy carries him through the unknown. And that's the lesson for all of us: Once you step into your purpose, the obstacles won't disappear, but you will be equipped to ride them.

As we've all heard, it's lonely at the top. A majority of C-suite leaders I've spoken to have said or intimated that fear has driven them to succeed, which blew my mind.

*Fear of what?*

I have to wonder: What are they, the masters of their craft and on top of their game, afraid of?

They fear not hitting their numbers.

If they don't hit their numbers, they may lose their job, and that is real for many.

Over the years, I've coached leaders to reframe that mindset.

Let's say you are the president of one of the top beauty brands in the world. Rather than being constantly afraid of missing the trend, not understanding your audience, not making your numbers, what if you stepped into why you entered the beauty and wellness industry in the first place?

Many people work in these industries because they enjoy giving hope and confidence to their customers when they show up in life. Now that's a thought someone can get excited about! And that is a great purpose.

Creating hope and confidence for your customers and honoring your decades-long track record of success should make anyone excited! You can connect your products with as many customers as possible, and this will help position them in their purpose.

I have also found that when people bring that excitement and enthusiasm with them rather than fear, they have a much higher likelihood of achieving all their goals and then some.

They'll also enjoy overall health and balance, which limits one's tendency for the chronic illness, stress, and injuries that come as a result of fight or flight raising one's cortisol levels. So many executives today that I speak with have chronic pain (I was one of them!) after living and working in constant fight or flight.

When one adopts an abundance mindset, there is no room for fear. No room for stress and anxiety.

What Kelly Slater has learned is how to turn his fear into a challenge—one that his mind and body are up for and open to.

When he does that, he transforms or, better yet, metamorphosizes his fear into energy, and that positive energy takes him wherever he wants to go.

When we learn to identify and harness feelings, we can use them as fuel for the journey. Once you step out into the great wide open of your purpose, you aren't going to necessarily have it easy. Every person who is on a path following their purpose knows that it comes with dangers, fears, failures, mistakes, outside forces, uncertainty, and change.

Yet stepping into your purpose won't necessarily be easy. When Kelly Slater was hit in the head by his own board in France and sank below the water, unconscious, he woke up afraid. He had no idea where he was or the direction he'd been swimming—toward the surface or away from it. If he had panicked and let fear overwhelm him in that moment, he would have died. But he kept swimming and following where his intuition took him. He broke the surface, got some air, and rode the rest of the waves in to shore and safety.

Following your purpose will require you to become adept at listening to your body, your energy, and the energy of the world around you—and also to tap into it. You'll need to be able to distinguish what makes you happy, joyful, content, and alive from what makes you feel depleted, afraid, and cut off from your inner voice and intuition.

That tension you feel before launching the new project, writing the deck, stepping into the unknown? That's your version of the waves Kelly rides.

The fear will come. The doubt will whisper. But so will the flow—*if you listen.*

Don't wait for perfect. Don't wait until you "feel ready." The wave is already rising. Drop in.

ACTIVITY

## Plan To Take On the World with Love, Not Fear

Before you begin, know this: Writing things down and journaling is more than reflection—it's a form of release. Like crying or screaming, writing moves energy out of your body and into the world. It turns thoughts into motion. It makes healing real. This activity doesn't require a notebook, but if anything comes up—write it down. Part of the growth is being able to witness your own evolution in real time.

First, sit quietly for 5 or 10 minutes, until you feel settled and neutral. When you are ready, ask your body two questions:

Is my [purpose, job, relationship, etc.] coming from love or fear? Where do I feel it?

Then ask these follow-ups:

If I feel expansive and love, what other activities can I do to further this feeling? What is the next right step I can take to keep this feeling going?

If I begin to feel fear, is it a legitimate fear? For example, think of entering an ocean with 50-foot waves that could drown you, versus going to a work event where you will have to get uncomfortable and put yourself out there in a different way?

Am I looking for excuses not to go or do something that is on my journey to living my purpose? Am I using past experiences to rationalize away positive future ones? Am I willing to transform this fear into excitement so I can do something I've never done before?

How do I feel after I transform my fear into excitement? Do I still feel anxious and constricted? If so, then this [purpose, job, relationship, etc.] may not be for me.

## Chapter 3

# Fan the Flames

## *Understanding the Interplay of Passion and Purpose*

> Success is not about winning or losing, it's about being true to yourself and living a life of purpose.
>
> —Quincy Jones

Can you imagine a world without Michael Jackson's *Thriller*? Or what about the biggest charity single of all time, the four-time Grammy-winning "We Are the World"? When musical legends such as Bruce Springsteen, Ray Charles, Diana Ross, Bob Dylan, Tina Turner, Billy Joel, and Lionel Richie, among many more, came together to raise money to fight poverty and hunger in Africa? What about the movie *The Color Purple* or the popular '90s TV show *The Fresh Prince of Bel-Air* starring Will Smith? None of these wildly successful albums, songs, collaborations, movies, or television shows would have happened without one man living out his purpose: Quincy Jones Jr.

To me, Quincy Jones epitomizes someone who sparked his passion, found his purpose, and achieved the impossible. He is an absolute legend. It's why we chose him as a PTTOW! Icon. My entire childhood was defined by his music. He created an entirely new genre of music. There is not one area of music today—from pop to folk to funk to jazz to hip-hop to rap—that hasn't had some influence that can point back to Quincy in some form.

When I think of people who inspired youth culture, Quincy Jones is at the top of my list. And when I think of people who literally embodied what it means to live your purpose, I think of Quincy Jones. He passed away while I was writing this book, and when I heard the news, my first thought was about how he broke every mold. He changed the world—he changed me. He helped me understand and find my purpose.

Many people think their purpose has to be tied to service or helping others. That's noble and good, but that's not what our purpose is. "Purpose" is semantics; it can mean different things to different people.

It might not be what you think. First, let's pin down what I mean by "purpose" in this book. Purpose is a question—actually, it's a series of related questions:

*Why am I here on this earth?*

*Why was I born?*

*What am I supposed to be doing here on this physical, earthly experience?*

*What's the point of all this?*

*What am I meant to do?*

To find the answers, we have to tap into our feelings. When you feel energy running through your body, you enter a flow state, and the feeling of time stopping. A word of caution: Many of us mistake flow for being on autopilot—doing things out of habit. Flow is different from autopilot. It's not like driving somewhere and realizing you can't remember how you got there. Flow is the opposite: It's being hyper-present in every moment, so present that time feels like it disappears.

*Our purpose is that thing inside us that makes us come alive, that reveals our soul to us and to others.*

It's usually *not* what our parents or loved ones expect or encourage us to be—doctors, lawyers, bankers, and so forth.

Our purpose often defies logic and calls us to step outside our comfort zone. Yet when we engage in an activity related to our purpose, even when it's difficult, we feel compelled to keep going. Our body and soul can feel that it's right.

You know it when you feel it. It's the excitement you felt when you were a child, the freedom. The feeling of expansion, joy. Giddiness, elation.

Purpose feels like love, not fear. That's not to say pursuing our purpose isn't scary. After all, it can be terrifying to defy your parents' expectations, your own ideas of "what you should be doing," or the lives you see friends and colleagues leading. The thing is, our true purpose often doesn't make sense at first, especially to others looking at our lives from the outside.

Finding your purpose, then, shouldn't be conflated with all the external trappings of success. For me, true success means staying true to your own values and aspirations and pursuing a life that is aligned with your purpose. You can have all the money and titles in the world, but if you're miserable, time feels like it's stuck, and you feel disconnected from yourself, then you're not living your purpose.

Think of your purpose as your pilot light. It lights you from the inside, and it's always there burning inside you. It's your job to keep that fire lit and continually fan the flame. But how do you do that?

*By doing the very thing you were destined to do.*

It's easy to take for granted that Quincy Jones is who he is, because of all he has managed to achieve. Some might argue it was sheer talent—or his access to some of the most brilliant minds in the music industry throughout his career. But it all started with a passion and a purpose.

I've had the privilege of spending time with Quincy on several occasions over the years and was especially inspired by his origin story. Quincy was just a boy who fell in love with music when he was in elementary school, born to a brilliant, musically talented mother who spoke several languages and a father who was a master carpenter. You might think he became so successful because of his parents' positive influence. But his childhood was far from ideal. Quincy was surrounded by gangsters and criminals. The streets were tough, and he had no safe haven. Wherever he looked, he saw terrifying characters and no way out. Even at home, he felt unsafe. Quincy's mother suffered from a vitamin B deficiency and slowly lost her mental faculties. Eventually, Quincy's father was forced to put her in a mental health treatment facility.

Before his mother was institutionalized—when Quincy was just seven—he used to love to hear his mother sing to him. Music lit her up from the inside. After his mother left, Quincy would sit and listen to his neighbor play the piano through the wall. He felt an irresistible pull. Then one day he walked into his neighbor's apartment and sat down to play. He was a natural, or as his neighbor recalled when she saw him play for the first time, "Music was in his soul."

*He had found a passion.*

Musical talent may have been something he was born with, but it's what he did with that passion that made all the difference. During the Great Depression, his father took his family from Chicago to find work in the naval yards of Seattle, Washington. There, Quincy had to hustle and rely on his wits to survive.

He also found refuge in the Armory—a local recreation center that he once broke into with his brother while scavenging for food. One night, after filling up on ice cream and pie, he wandered into a stage area that was furnished with a piano. At just 11 years old, Quincy sat down and began to make music. After that, he never stopped. Something had clicked inside. He knew this was what he was put on earth to do. Time disappeared.

*He had found his purpose.*

As for many iconic figures, music was an escape for Quincy. He needed a place to feel safe, and in music he found it. Shortly after, he joined choir and band at school. He learned every instrument he could. By the time he entered high school he had joined a band with his friend Ray Charles and fell in love with the trumpet. But he wasn't only escaping the streets; he was writing and arranging.

Quincy's story reminds us that no one rises alone. His journey required teachers, mentors, and collaborators—proof that greatness multiplies when shared. That's the DNA of PTTOW!: bringing people together to do the NBDB.

> I've learned that the only way to keep my flame bright is abandoning myself completely to every moment I'm alive.
>
> —Quincy Jones

Once you start fanning the flames, you can do anything you set your mind to. You can achieve more than you ever imagined. By fanning the flames of our passions, we are able to push past any self-imposed limitations, build confidence, find success, and ultimately reach unknown heights. Aligning with and fanning the flames of your purpose is the key that unlocks every barrier. It unleashes an enormous power that essentially makes the impossible possible.

You may not be producing *Thriller* . . . yet. But maybe you're leading a 150-person team through chaos, building a category, or trying to scale culture as fast as you're scaling revenue.

Maybe your passion's buried under investor decks and hiring decisions, but it's still there, quietly asking, *"Are we building something real? Something that moves people?"*

Quincy didn't become Quincy because he chased hits.

He sat at the piano every day—not for the applause, but because he *had to.*

So ask yourself: What's the thing you'd build even if no one invested?

That's your purpose. Fan that flame.

---

ACTIVITY

## Fan the Flames—Understanding the Interplay of Passion and Purpose

This activity has several parts. Take your time and respond to the prompts in your journal. This work was integral in my own life, and I have seen it work wonders with PTTOW! members who were searching for their own purpose.

I'm going to take you through the process of getting in the ballpark of your purpose. At worst, this exercise will help confirm that you are on the right path of your purpose. At best, it will help you make an adjustment and step into what's most true for you.

### Step 1: Feel Your Purpose

What is purpose? It's a feeling. Just like love isn't a thought, it's a feeling. Know that your purpose is when you are in flow, "in the zone," when time seemingly slows down or stops, and you don't know where the time went.

Some of you may be stumped. How do I know if what I am obsessed about is just a fleeting passion, a whim, and not really my purpose? I'll make this easy for you. If you've been thinking about it for years—it's your purpose. Passions fizzle. Lust fades. Infatuations flatten. They come and they go—they don't keep you up at night. They don't nag you at bedtime. They don't keep you thinking, *What if I could do it?* Another way to think of it is that passion is something that sits on the surface, but purpose feels embodied—it's ongoing. You can't shake it. (For some, purpose may last 5–10 years, and then we evolve, change as humans. That's why we hear about the seven-year itch. For others, it may stay with them their entire lives.)

Passion is excitement, thrill, a burst of euphoria. It can be used to fuel purpose, but it isn't purpose. It's the energy necessary for you to fulfill your purpose.

*Purpose* is a full-bodied *yes*. It's knowing, *This is what I am supposed to be doing, and I can't do anything else—even when it's hard, harder than anything I've ever done.*

I'm passionate and excited about music, but I know that my purpose isn't to be in the music industry. I love to dance. Go to clubs. Travel to hear my favorite artists. Sit in the audience and be awed and inspired. None of that has anything to do with my purpose, though. I'm passionate about movies, but I know my life's work isn't in the movie industry. I'm passionate about mountain biking and cycling the streets of Miami, but it's not my purpose.

*Your purpose is your craft, your life's work. Your passion is the matches, the kindling, and the logs that keep you fueled and energized, and your purpose is the fire—that burns bright inside you. It's a constant for a steady amount of time.*

*For me, my Purpose is to experience Awe and Wonder. How do I know? Because I get that type of feeling whenever I experience something new, like an invention, technology, performance art, concerts, movies, and theatrical experiences.*

## Step 2: Follow the Breadcrumbs

Now grab your journal. For this creative exercise, put aside your present life and career. Pretend it doesn't exist. Otherwise your ego will want to be right and justify that you're on the correct path.

Close your eyes. Think back to when you were six, seven, eight years old. What did you love to do when no one was looking? What did you do that made time stand still and hours pass in moments? That made you giddy with excitement for no apparent reason? Don't judge yourself for whatever comes up. I want you to think about what *you* wanted before your parents, friends, grandparents, and teachers projected, in the most loving way, what they wanted for you. Write all this down.

From that moment to where you are today, think of the activities you did in your life that seemed to stop time. Think in increments of five years. Where did time seem to stop? Was there a hobby you pursued in your free time that you loved? What were the most exciting parts of your job? Write those moments down. Try to bring them together like collecting breadcrumbs on a path that leads to your destination. Is there any throughline coursing across your life? Write that down.

Here's an example:

*My favorite movie is* Moulin Rouge, *and I know more about the history of the circus than most people do, so experiencing Awe and Wonder landed for me when thinking of all the times that time began to stop for me. I remember how time stopped when I first walked into the nosebleed section of Anaheim Stadium for a big game and again at 14 years old to see Michael Jackson perform. I almost had a "white out." Everything stopped, and I felt a sense of energy, even oneness. Later, at 26 years old, to get over a breakup I went to Magic School at the Magic Castle. At 36 years old, I hosted my first event at Cirque du Soleil, and ever since then have been on every one of the Cirque resident shows in Las Vegas at PTTOW! We have a WOW team, whose job it is to make our members say: Wow! We have some of the world's best magicians, including David Blaine, David Copperfield, or Oz Pearlman, as part of our community.*

## Step 3: Step Out of the Shadow Role

Some of us play smaller than we're capable of. We stay in the shadows—not because we don't have talent, tenacity, or vision, but because stepping forward feels risky. I call this the "Shadow Role."

It might look like hiding behind a title, staying in support mode when you're ready to lead, or keeping your creativity quiet because it feels safer than putting it out there. But here's the truth: You don't always need to quit your job or change your career to step out of the shadows. Often, it's about bringing more of yourself, and more of what gives you energy, into the role you already have. Speaking up, sharing your ideas, taking that bold step that makes your value visible.

So ask yourself: Where in your life and work are you dimming your own brilliance, and how can you spend more time on the work that fuels you instead of the work that drains you? What are you afraid of stepping into? Now write that down.

I had my "aha!" moment of seeing my Shadow Role after doing this exercise. After over two decades of diving into the world of economics, business, profit and loss statements, and finance, I realized that my Shadow Role was finance and business. If I stepped into the full fire of my Purpose, then I would be the main character, get out of my comfort zone, and become the CEO, Creator, Founder, and Main-Stage Speaker. Today, my Purpose is to be the CEO and leader of PTTOW! I've been a CEO for nearly 20 years. I love directing my energy to those things that bring vitality and excitement into my life, rather than going through all the same old motions, year after year. I may not love dealing with legal, human resources, or finance, but I enjoy working with and coaching our team, being there for our members, and traveling the world to find talents and experiences that help curate our community. I began to road-map my role as the CEO to give more time and energy to those things, versus to functions that depleted me.

Creating a road map for your role in your current job or career is an ideal way to shift into the things that will excite you the most and thus make you better at what you do, while delivering more value to everyone around you.

## Step 4: Combine All the Parts

1. What puts you into flow state?
2. What were your "aha!" moments when you followed the breadcrumbs of your life?
3. What's your Shadow Role?

Combining all three answers gives us clues to what we truly feel called to be.

Now, I want you to consider the answers to those three questions in Step 2: What did you want to do when you were six, seven, eight years old? What are the activities that you pursue that you love and time seems to just disappear? Is there any overlap or gap between where you are (your current role) and where you want to be?

Follow those breadcrumbs all the way through where you are today. Can you connect the dots? I'll bet when you do, you will have an "aha!" moment too. It will either reinforce the path you're currently on to help you find your purpose or reveal that you need to make adjustments to get from where you are to where you need to be. The following chapters will help you work through those adjustments.

# Chapter 4

# Identify and Nurture Your Natural Talents

> Great performance is in our hands far more than most of us ever suspected.
>
> —Geoff Colvin, *Talent Is Overrated: What Really Separates World-Class Performers from Everybody Else*

I've found that most people who are able to do what's NBDB recognized their talent early on. This talent usually aligned with something they were passionate about. However, as alluded to last chapter, many of us leave that part of us behind when we are kids to pursue things that might be more socially acceptable (i.e., pays the bills, is a safe job). All of us have a natural talent—something only *we* possess in our families and are inclined to do. Ever since I was a boy, I wanted to be a "part of the show," and as a cofounder of PTTOW! in many ways I am nurturing that natural talent to bring people together and put on a spectacular show.

I believe everyone has a gift—and it's our job to nurture it, or as I like to call it, "fan the flames" of it—just as my friend, world-renowned snowboard champion, and PTTOW! Icon Shaun White had done. After spending time with him over the years, I would go so far as to say he was *engulfed in it.*

From the outset, Shaun White's parents knew that their son was no ordinary boy. He was born with tetralogy of Fallot, a congenital heart disorder, sometimes referred to as a "hole in the heart" that accompanies three other conditions. By the time he was a year old, Shaun had endured two open-heart surgeries to correct the defects. When you've already stared down mortality before you can even walk, fear takes on a different shape. Maybe that's why Shaun approached life with such an uncanny willingness to go for it.

While this condition can be critical, even fatal if not treated early on, it didn't seem to affect Shaun as it did others. In fact, it may have helped him. With nothing to lose—having experienced close brushes with death before he even reached the age of consciousness—he seemed to come out of the experiences with an uncanny ability to face down the barrel of life with absolutely no fear.

According to his parents, Shaun was never afraid—ever. Nothing slowed him down.

Shaun, however, remembers it differently—he recalls feeling his knees shake the first time he dropped into his first snowboarding competition. But even though he experienced the fear, he didn't let it stop him. That tension—fear in his knees, courage in his heart—would become the hallmark of his career.

*He just kept going.*

He was driven from a young age to move—and move fast. And despite the heart condition, he seemed born a natural athlete. He followed his older brother, Jesse, everywhere, especially the skate park, where legends like Tony Hawk showed off their most daring tricks.

Shaun was a fast study. He was able to mimic what his brother, Hawk, and others were doing on their boards and quickly pick it up. Soon he was competing right alongside skaters three times his age.

On the weekends, Shaun and his family left the skateboards in the garage and headed to the mountains of San Bernardino to snowboard. They didn't have much money—just enough to hit the slopes—so they often slept in their van. Shaun ate, breathed, and slept boarding, snow or skate. A board seemed to be an extension of him, like an arm or a leg. He has admitted on more than one occasion he doesn't know who he would be without the boards. He knew he was born to do this. And it's all he wanted to do. So that is exactly what he did. He kept at it. Had he been a natural who never practiced, pushed himself, tried, failed, fell, and got back up again, he wouldn't be the Shaun White we all know. This is a reminder that talent might open the door, but a healthy obsession keeps you walking through it.

Because his family quickly realized he possessed a natural—some might say supernatural—ability, they began entering him into competitions and helping him practice. By the time he was just 7, he'd landed his first sponsorship. When he was 13, he was placing in professional snowboarding events—alongside men nearly a decade his senior. Many weren't exactly happy to be competing against a "kid," aka a prodigy—and getting smoked by him.

Within three years, he was a millionaire and becoming a household name—not just in the snowboarding community but also in the burgeoning world of extreme sports. He was thrust onto the world stage in 2006, when he took home the Olympic gold medal at Torino. He again won gold in 2010 in Vancouver.

Shaun wasn't done. What most people don't know is that while Shaun was crushing it on the mountains during the Winter Olympics, he was also competing on skateboard in the X Games. After winning gold in Torino in 2006, he then received the gold in the

2007 X Games, followed by an X Games bronze in 2008 and silver in 2010. And then again after winning gold in the Vancouver Olympics in snowboarding, in 2011 he landed another gold in skateboarding at the Los Angeles X Games.

When most expected him to retire, Shaun began practicing for the 2018 PyeongChang Olympics.

Then tragedy struck.

While preparing for the games in New Zealand, he attempted a back-to-back double cork 1440 (in which one spins twice and flips four times). He missed his landing and slammed his head and upper body into the superpipe. His face ripped open. He needed more than 60 facial stitches and couldn't even look at himself in the mirror. His lungs were injured so badly and were filling with blood so quickly, he was forced to spit it into a bucket. This was his crucible moment—the place where natural talent bowed to grit, obsession, and purpose. Facing the lowest of the lows, and even the realization he might never compete again, Shaun kept asking himself: *What can I learn from this? How can I be made better by it?*

And that's exactly what he did. He decided not only to get better physically but mentally too. Determined to make it to the 2018 Winter Olympics in PyeongChang, Shaun had to kick it into high gear—because what once came naturally to him didn't. He wasn't flipping as fast. Things slowed down. So he slowed down. He had always worked hard, but now he was supercharging his workouts with a renewed sense of determination and an understanding of what went wrong. In other words, *he learned from his mistakes and applied hard work and dedication.*

Shaun, like so many greats, realized nature will only take you so far. At some point, he needed to realign his focus and intention. He was extremely dedicated and disciplined in his approach, practicing the run over and over on the halfpipe. For four months he returned to his roots—when he ate, breathed, and slept boarding, like he did at the skatepark as a boy. That work paid off—he qualified. But when he dropped into the halfpipe on his second run, he fell.

It would be hard for anyone to shake off such a fall—especially after being injured so badly on a prior attempt. But Shaun wasn't giving up. On his third and final run, he landed the seemingly impossible and achieved the NBDB—a frontside double-cork 1440 and cab double-cork 1440 combo. Once again, Shaun made history—and took home another gold for the USA. In that moment, Shaun proved something greater than athletic dominance: Falling, bleeding, and failing are not the end; they are the price you pay for greatness.

Some have been left to wonder—was it Shaun's natural talent that made him the GOAT in the snowboarding world? Or was it his dedication and hard work? To that Shaun would say it was a bit of both. But what I find most interesting is he doesn't attribute his success to either of those; rather, he credits his love of skateboarding—the reason he started to love boarding at all—with fueling and sustaining him, especially in the off seasons. As Shaun said in an interview with *Experience Life* magazine in 2023, "When you get consumed by something, like the way I was with snowboarding and skateboarding, it's an amazing feeling to just lose yourself and get *fully engulfed in it* [emphasis mine] . . . I don't think I would have continued to be a professional snowboarder if it hadn't been for skateboarding. You have to have that balance; you have to have other interests in your life."*

In the end, for Shaun, it was the love of what he originally had a talent in—skateboarding—that sustained him. Yes, he was a natural and leaned into it, but he also nurtured that talent with hard work, dedication, and putting all his heart and soul into his craft. He also

* Michael Dregni, "Shaun White: From Snowboarding Legend to Mentor and Entrepreneur," *Experience Life*, December 19, 2023.

fanned the flames of his natural passion and obsession. As he said himself, he became "fully engulfed" in his love of boarding—snow or skate. That's what being in your Purpose means. Watching Shaun live engulfed in his purpose reminds me of why we built PTTOW!—to fan the flames of talent and passion until they ignite something bigger than ourselves.

---

ACTIVITY

## Plan To Take On the World Using Your Natural Gift

Spend some time thinking and journaling about your natural gifts by responding to the following prompts:

1. Do you know what your natural talents are?
2. If you do, how do you nurture them? Do you practice them or test them out?
3. If you are struggling to identify your natural talent, what do you feel you are naturally inclined to do? Or what do you seem to excel at more than others?
4. Does your natural talent align with your passions? For example, Shaun White was passionate about and talented in both skate- and snowboarding. Do you have something you are both passionate about and gifted at?

Chapter 5

# Get Out of Your Routine to Be Inspired

> The best way to predict your future is to create it, not from the known, but from the unknown. When the mind is open to the unknown, it can imagine all possibilities.
>
> —Dr. Joe Dispenza

I can point to a few magical, prescient moments in my life. One of them for me was a phone call that changed everything.

When I set out to create PTTOW!, I was met with so much resistance. Everyone around me I trusted told me it was a horrible idea—there was no money to be made and there was no definitive audience or niche. And there was no way I—Roman Tsunder—was going to be able to get the big names I was hoping to attract to our events. Who did I think I was, trying to get someone like the Dalai Lama to show up? What, was I just going to call him up and say, "Hey, I'd love for you to come and talk to my small gathering of folks who want to impact youth culture"?

Yes, that's exactly what I did.

*Sort of.*

As these things go, I had some connections—and those connections over time became friendships. I was just being me, Roman, and befriending people. One of these friends, Kelly Smith, invited me to a lunch in Laguna Beach, and to my right sat a Buddhist monk, Lama Tenzin, who I came to discover was the Dalai Lama's personal Emissary for Peace.

I knew the Dalai Lama enjoyed speaking to students at universities, so I went for it.

I asked, "Lama Tenzin, you know how His Holiness likes to speak to students at universities?"

"Yes," he replied.

"And you know how those students wear jeans and sweaters?"

"Yes," he said nodding in agreement.

"And you know how His Holiness is on Facebook and Twitter?"

Again, he nodded and said, "Yes, he recently met the founders of those companies."

So I went for it. "Wouldn't it be a great idea for him to speak to the leaders who make all those products?"

He paused for a minute and said he would meditate on it. I was not sure what to make of that, but I called Lama Tenzin a month later and asked if he had meditated on it.

He said, "Yes," and he thought what I was doing was a good idea.

"Great news, but what does that mean?" I inquired.

"I will speak to the Dalai Lama next time I go to Dharamshala, India, where the Dalai Lama lives."

Well, months passed and I had asked him several times if the Dalai Lama might be interested in coming to one of our summits.

He always responded that he simply said he hadn't had time to bring it up to him. Who could blame him? PTTOW! wasn't even a real company, and at this point, mind you, I didn't think it would be anything more than a one-time event. After all, I was well versed in rejection. My early life as an immigrant and trying to make it on Wall Street had me used to hearing "No." I just kept working, kept trying. I believed in me. I knew what I could do. I knew what my purpose was—and I knew I could share it with others.

I was still struggling to get PTTOW! off the ground, But that wasn't all. I had left the company I founded (Access 360 Media, in 2009) to start a business called Mob Mobile. It was one of the most stressful periods in my life. Leaving the comforts and success of my prior company, to chase what I thought was a great idea, only to have it not work out. Suddenly, I found myself without a passion or a paycheck. It was destabilizing emotionally and financially. And since people told me that PTTOW! was a bad idea, I never took it seriously as a real business. So I felt rudderless . . . hopeless.

To make ends meet, I joined one of my friends who worked at Venture Fund in 2011. That summer my boss, Mark, invited me along on a yacht he had chartered off the coast of Croatia. When he asked me to join him, my first thought was, *This is the last thing that I should be doing right now—going on vacation*. This was so not me. Go on a trip and leaving all my work, connections, and stress behind? But my boss said, "I'm your boss right now, and I'm paying for it. So you're going."

This was a big leap for me. I let all the fears and worries go—and let myself believe I might be able to pull off PTTOW! What if instead of spending three months of work and passion on PTTOW! I spent all year on it and could I simply pay my bills and survive?

Fast-forward six months and I am on the phone with Lama Tenzin again—we had become friends by then. We talked for nearly 45 minutes and were wrapping up our conversation. I had stopped bugging him about the Dalai Lama a while ago. But something inside me said this is it: *Roman, just go for it.* I took the leap of faith and asked: "By the way, did you ever ask His Holiness about PTTOW!" And he responded, "Oh yes! He says what you are doing is a good thing!"

I literally fell to the ground. *The Dalai Lama knows about PTTOW! And he thinks it's a good thing?*

Up until that moment I had been losing my hair, I was gaunt from worry and stress, and I couldn't believe someone, let alone the Dalai Lama, believed in me and what I was trying to do. So I said, "Should I reserve the Penthouse Suite at the Ritz Carlton for His Holiness then?" Lama Tenzin replied, "Yes, that is a good idea."

At that moment, I realized His Holiness the Dalai Lama was coming to PTTOW! and it was only three months away! Even for a Jewish guy like me, His Holiness believing in my dream seemed like a good sign. So I decided to go for it and commit my life to it.

Looking back now, I realize the key to all of this wasn't the call itself. And it wasn't even the trip.

Those were all a construct—a story.

But, really, the past 15 years have given me a profound insight into that time. For years I have told the story of "serendipity"—a call that followed a leap of faith. That's just one side of the story. I actually had been working my ass off for years. I was so stressed and overwhelmed. There was nothing magical about losing my hair from all the stress. I don't think I truly understood what it meant to be still. In fact, I now know I was probably responding to everything happening in those days with a fight-or-flight reaction.

What I now remember was the power and profoundness of being still.

By going to Croatia, I stepped out of my day-to-day routine. It took me a while, but around day three, I got out of my own head. I let myself "be." I let go of figuring out what my next "big" company would be and focusing on the total addressable market or the business model. I let go of things not working out. I let myself enjoy the moment I was in. I mean, I was on a yacht off Croatia and someone else was paying for it? Why the hell not enjoy it? And so I let myself do just that. I let the new sights, sounds, smells, experiences, and people inspire me.

And that's what it means to be inspired. It means to be "in spirit" or in flow by experiencing that energy coming through you. And that's what we all need: NEW sights, sounds, smells, tastes. You are NOT going to be inspired in the same places you go day in and day out, or by taking the same drive you take home, or hanging out with the same friends.

Standing out on the bow of the yacht, looking out over the crystalline turquoise waters, I felt transformed. The sun was on my face as I marveled at this beautiful, extraordinary moment. And just like that, I was out of my own head, out of my own body. All the worries, fears, and self-doubt that had been eating away at me seemed to just go *Poof!* and were gone. It was just me: Roman. The construct of the world I found myself in was gorgeous, wonderful, surreal, impossible. *I was possible.* The word *impossible* literally spells *I'm possible!* It became so clear to me—as clear as the sea floor below me in this spectacular place.

And you may be wondering: *How could that be? What had changed?* Oh, just about everything. I was surrounded by new sights, new sounds, and new smells. It was all new. Every sensation, every experience, was forcing me literally to *be present.* And just as I had learned to be present with my experiences inside my body, I was able to track all the experiences outside my body. I was able to see the wonder and beauty of the gorgeous Croatian coast. I was able to be present with my friends.

Outside of my day-to-day routine, I was seeing things with a new set of eyes, hearing things with new ears, feeling sensations in a way I hadn't been able to feel them before. All the subconscious self-limiting beliefs seemed to get quiet, and the autopilot I was usually running on (that had one speed: GO) seemed to stop. I was getting still, quiet, and as a result present and inspired. I was being exposed to new people and ideas—people no more qualified or talented or experienced than me—doing things they loved. And for the first time, I thought, *Why not try PTTOW!? What if I was just able to survive?*

From that one instance of presence and stillness, I was able to throw aside all the naysayers. I cannot emphasize how important getting calm and present is when trying to achieve the impossible. It is the secret sauce. The special ingredient. It is what makes all things possible, because in that moment of stillness, worlds are created—your future is created. And when you do step into your purpose, into the thing that makes you come alive, serendipitous, magical things will happen that you can never put into a business plan. And I think that is my favorite part of finding and stepping into your purpose—getting everything you didn't know you wanted. The universe surprises and rewards you for having the courage to take that leap of faith.

It was also the first time I understood the saying that "what is meant for you is right under your nose and you may not even see it." I used to laugh at that saying. I'm not an idiot—if something was right under my nose, I would see it! Hello?

Well, I didn't.

PTTOW! was right under my nose for two years before that fateful trip to Croatia. It took stepping out of my day-to-day to finally see what my heart had already chosen: that I was meant to dive into this.

(Spoiler alert: It happened again—this time, with love. Turns out, the two most important things in my life were right under my nose: PTTOW! and my girlfriend, Teresa.)

But you may be wondering: What if I don't have friends who take me to Croatia? Where am I supposed to go to get still?

Well, what if I told you, you could experience what I did anywhere, at any time? That all exists within you too?

I didn't know it then. I hadn't yet learned the power of meditation, or met the Dalai Lama. I just knew what being present felt like. It was a clearing, a stillness, a return to the perfection of my soul, where all things seemed possible.

Whenever you close your eyes and breathe, noting the inhale and the exhale, or force yourself to stop and pay attention to the sights, sounds, and sensations all around you, you are becoming still and present. It's the moment when you allow your true self to emerge—not the person from the past, with regrets, mistakes, heartaches, and traumas, or the person in the future with all the worries and fears that come with it. That's what Buddhists call the monkey mind running wild. In the present, there's just you, sitting with all the awe and wonder. You can do this in your backyard, your kitchen, your bed, on the bus, in your car. All you have to do to get still is to *be still*—that means be present. You can actually be still while walking, running, gardening, hiking, or sitting in a café and talking with a friend.

And when I mean still, I mean *present*. Locked in. Just you and the moment. I would encourage you to get out of your known and familiar day-to-day environment. Leave your city and go on a hike, road trip, to the beach, any place that calls to you and allows you to get out of your head and day-to-day routine.

Ironically, being present, still, and slow is the fastest way to go anywhere. If you want to go fast, go slow. Slow is smooth and smooth is fast. So many of us have been lied to all our lives about slow. We were told that hustling and grinding and working around the clock is the only way to succeed. We don't stop enough, rest enough, recharge enough.

Now hear me when I say that this is not permission to phone it in. Being still and present does not mean doing your job poorly or cutting corners. I am not advocating logging off at 5 PM sharp and leaving your colleagues hanging on important projects. I believe in doing your work well and putting in the hours. I still believe that you should take pride in what you do and have integrity in what you do. After all, "work is love made visible." What I mean by being present and still is being intentional, mindful, and methodical.

What I am giving you is permission to slow down—to do one thing at a time. Trust that you have the talent and skills to do the work in front of you. You don't have to hustle and grind when you're in flow with your purpose; you simply flow. You'll feel less anxiety, no stress, no fear. There is just you and what you're meant to do.

I often meet entrepreneurs who are in the hustle-and-grind mindset. They tell me about the three or four companies they are building or advising or investing in. I think mostly it sounds like being busy, and all that busy-ness is usually a red flag. When I look at some of the most successful company leaders like Jeff Bezos, Mark Zuckerberg, Whitney Wolfe Herd, Tim Cook, Payal Kadakia, or Jensen Huang, they have devoted a significant part of their lives to just one company, at least at a time.

When you let go—some call it surrender—and stop fighting doing the work, resisting what is happening, complaining about what's not working, arguing for your limitations, blaming others for your failures, you can just stop and notice and appreciate all that is going right in the world, in you, in the moment, the perfect present moment, all the good and amazing things from this moment.

Another mentor and inspiration of mine who has mastered the ability to let go is Dr. Joe Dispenza, who has led think tanks at PTTOW!. He teaches our members and those who read his books that we can change our reality in this present moment. He argues that to create any new outcome or reality, you need to break the habits that have made you, and this requires changing your state of mind. To change your current reality, you need to change your thoughts, which trigger your emotions. For example, when you tell and retell a story that makes you feel angry, upset, frustrated, or stressed—those repeated thoughts trigger the same emotions, conditioning your body to stay in that state. If you stop telling the story, and reframe it or begin a new one, you create a new feeling. This feeling is what creates a new outcome. When you close your eyes and visualize your future when you are in a positive-feeling present emotion, amazing things can happen. You'll make good decisions in a positive, present state. And a positive future awaits; as Joe Dispenza says, "Your personal reality becomes your personality." The thoughts and feelings you exude help determine the life that you magnetize.

---

ACTIVITY

## Plan To Take On the World Vibe Check

If you want to Plan To Take On the World, then plan on getting your emotions in a positive state (good vibes only!). How do you do that? Work backward. Address your thoughts by asking what old stories you are committed to or that you keep telling over and over:

- What is a current habit of yours that you do not love?
- How would you like to use that time for a different and better habit?
- Is the choice, acquaintance, or decision at the center of this habit that I'm about to make bringing me closer to or further from the person who I want to be? This is a question I often

like to ask myself, and the practice is easy. If the answer is yes, you do it! If it's no, then you do the hard thing by taking a different action that will bring yourself closer to who you want to be.

- Try a complaint/blame/old-story detox. Can you stop complaining, blaming, and beating the drum of the same old negative stories for a week, two weeks, a month? See what happens!
- Be intentional with your time. Seek out moments of awe and wonder, appreciation, gratitude, joy, and abundance in the present moment. Try to do this for a week, two weeks, a month. See what happens—no Croatian cruise necessary.

Chapter 6

# Do Shadow Work to Embrace Your Whole Self

> One does not become enlightened by imagining figures of light, but by making the darkness conscious.
>
> —Carl Jung

Many of you know you could be doing more. But others may see something else at play. Perhaps, from another's perspective, you seem to have everything going for you—*living a life most people would envy.* Perhaps you arrived there through sheer grit and hard work. You defied all the odds to get where you are, but nothing about what you're doing fires you up. That elusive state of flow never clicks in.

If either scenario exists, you have to have a deep talk with your *Shadow Self* and do what's called *Shadow Work*.

But first let me clarify what this Shadow Self is (and what it's not). It's not your "dark side" (i.e., your bad side), as it's often misunderstood and mischaracterized. I tend to think your Shadow Self, once brought into the light and merged with your whole self, can be your super power.

Think of your bright, beautiful, shining soul holding up a shield to protect itself from incoming attacks in the outside world—trauma, rejection, abandonment, abuse, name calling, expectations, and so forth. What happens when you hold something out in front of you so the light can't come through? A shadow forms. The light (the soul) is there, but it can't shine as brightly, because part of it's covered in shadow.

The shield we put out in front is like a mask we wear to hide this part of ourselves. It takes its shapes through personalities, behaviors, beliefs, and even Shadow Roles that all serve to protect us from the glare of the outside world. The shadow that results protects your most authentic self from the world.

While your Shadow Self emerges to protect you at first, it becomes so dominant that many of us grow unaware of how much of our authenticity that shadow starts to block.

Shadow Work means exploring the parts of you that have been unconsciously blocking your self from receiving all the light you deserve.

All of us have parts of ourselves that we're proud of or that we know "work." But a lot of us repress or keep silent parts that we fear will be ridiculed or rejected. This fear of rejection can wreak havoc on your life and manifests itself in several ways. You can develop poor self-esteem, anxiety, or depression; succumb to self-sabotage or self-absorption (sometimes even narcissism); and overcompensate by growing an inflated ego. You may be someone (or know someone) who presents yourself as "living my best life," but it's just a mask you wear to convince yourself and the outside world. Deep down inside, you may be hurting.

Some of us are aware of our Shadow and try to reject it. This shows up as projection. You begin rejecting the very thing that you rejected in yourself or are blocking others from seeing. As a result, you judge others harshly—and this lack of compassion toward others is turned inward. You begin to unconsciously self-hate. All hatred is rooted in self-hatred. You don't have to look far to see how self-hatred and fear can be projected onto others. The seeds of racism, homophobia, antisemitism, and many more are planted in one's own self long before those hatreds are projected onto others. I'm never surprised to hear that some outspoken homophobe who loudly attacked gay rights was discovered to have had an extramarital affair with a person of their gender. In attempting to repress or hide their shadow self, they projected self-hatred on to others.

I have a friend who was told to not speak when she was young. It was unbecoming to be so outspoken, her mother told her. This, in turn, caused my very opinionated, outspoken, and chatty friend to retreat. She put up a shield to hide her spark from being exposed to the light. Even though she felt called to be onstage and out in front of people, she retreated to a world of books—never really finding her own voice until her late 30s. As she grew up, she was often annoyed by people who were outspoken and unafraid to be the center of attention. It wasn't until she did Shadow Work with a trusted therapist that she realized the very thing she was judging others for, she was hiding from the world. Her childhood self wanted to be onstage—a performer. She had big dreams of being out in front of, instead of hiding behind, the curtains on the stage of her own life.

Remember that your Shadow isn't a *monster living inside you that needs to be slayed*. You might think of it as the little child inside you who needs to be hugged and told, "You are fine just the way you are. You came into this world with natural gifts, talents, feelings, longings, and personalities you never needed to hide to make others comfortable, let alone feel safe." The main goal of Shadow Work is to be compassionate toward yourself. The work is really just to get curious about the parts of yourself you have been holding back.

Think of Shadow Work like parenting your younger self . . . say, your seven-year-old self. I call mine Little Roman. Feel free to name yours as well.

Recently, I was sitting in the audience of a private Andrea Bocelli performance in Italy. It was mind blowing. I was just in awe of the sheer talent and stage presence of so many magnetic and talented people. There was something so undeniable stirring inside me when I sat in the audience watching the spectacular production. Part of me said, "I don't want to be here in the audience. I want to be up there—a part of whatever that is—that wonderful, awe-inspiring, jaw-dropping, soul-filling experience."

Instead of being worried about this or even feeling envious of the performers' talents, I understood this longing was pointing to a natural calling. By doing Shadow Work, I am much more comfortable expressing parts of myself that I would never have dreamed of when I was a college student trying desperately to fit into the world of finance. Now when I do anything, I ask myself, *Would this impress Little Roman? Am I everything he hoped I'd be when he grew up? If not, then why not?*

And here is the wild thing about Shadow Work: After you do it, you don't need to throw away all that you learned in your Shadow Career or in those adopted personas and beliefs. Yes, sometimes they call you to step into the light, but that career and actions and beliefs got you to where you are today. You don't want to dismiss or throw them away. They are your tools, your prologue to the next and best chapter of your life.

One person I always think of in relation to Shadow Work is Omani Carson, the founder and chairman of Carson Group, a leading financial services company serving financial advisors and investors through its three businesses: Carson Wealth, Carson Coaching, and Carson Partners. Omani, a billionaire, is also a *New York Times* bestselling author, one of only two financial advisors ever inducted into the inaugural *Barron*'s Hall of Fame, an award-winning entrepreneur, a dynamic keynote speaker, and a passionate philanthropist.

Several years ago he began therapy to overcome a difficult and tumultuous childhood, marked by neglect, his mother's mental illness, and poverty. Through life-changing psychedelic therapy at the Carson Healing Ranch, Omani began to change inside. As a person who was an expert at making money, he was seeking ways to better help others. He became active in accelerating social and environmental change, hoping to "do the greatest amount of good for the greatest number of people."

He and his wife, Jeanie, cofounded the Dreamweaver Foundation, a nonprofit organization dedicated to "fulfilling end-of-life dreams for seniors with terminal illness." Omani also has formed partnerships with No Hungry Children and charity: water. Deeply affected by his mother, he also supports individuals enduring mental health challenges through various initiatives designed to help people transcend scarcity, isolation, and loneliness and achieve abundance by living out their full potential.

Now Omani's purpose is to discover and build the ultimate human experience, which will allow people to find and live their own purpose and live abundantly every day. Omani made his billions while working from his Shadow Self, where he learned all the skills and talents that made him successful. Now Omani has stepped into his whole self—where he's able to integrate his Shadow with his True Self and live his divine purpose—helping others transform too.

When you follow Omani's formula of Past Achievement (sometimes by way of Shadow Careers) and multiply it by Shadow Work, it produces a massive explosion of light that allows your whole self to shine like the dazzling star it is meant to be—illuminating all those around you and more. It moves you out of the dark and into the magnificent light.

***His Shadow Self Achievements × Shadow Work on the Shadow Self = Exponential Growth Not Just for Himself but Others as Well***

I like to think of doing Shadow Work as putting yourself in a slingshot or a rocket. Once you climb the first mountain and achieve all you think you can, then do Shadow Work, you are literally shot across to the Second Mountain (see chapter 15 for more on this topic). It's amazing how fast this process can help you grow and get where you want to go.

---

ACTIVITY

## What Is Hiding in Your Shadows?

Open your notebook and begin to answer or contemplate these questions. No one but you will be reading the answers. This process is only meant to bring awareness to the parts of you that you may need to embrace. No one is going to shame you. As a matter of fact, feel free to burn or throw this paper away once done. Be as honest as you can. See what comes to light. If you feel uncomfortable or overwhelmed, seek help from a therapist that specializes in Shadow Work to guide you. Remember to be compassionate with yourself.

1. Think about a time when someone may have shamed you for something you loved or enjoyed, and you may have hidden

it since from others. What do you think will happen if you bring this into the light?

2. What is something you would be so afraid of if it was revealed? Why? What do you think will happen?
3. What are some positive traits or activities that have resulted from your Shadow Self and Career? How can they help you become more authentic and real?
4. What would impress the young version of yourself (before you had to put up an armored shield that cast a shadow on you)?
5. What can you do today to impress this young version of yourself?

# Chapter 7

# Align Your Mind and Body

The body keeps the score.

—Bessel van der Kolk

I want you to think about this right now. *Your life is a dream*—it is happening and unfolding in every second of every day. What is past can't be undone or caught again. The future is unknowable. All we have, then, is the present, and our sensations, images, feelings, and thoughts. All that you have and all you will ever be is already happening—right now.

So what is consciousness? It's the awareness that we are. We, the human, form the physical entity, body and mind. Most of us, however, are completely unaware of our thoughts, let alone how they determine how we behave or feel day to day. We go about our lives totally in the Matrix.

Notice I didn't say, "*almost* in the Matrix." I said, "*totally* in the Matrix." Also known as *society* in my book. We get in our cars, drive to work, do what we're told, believe what we've been taught to believe, eat, go to bed, sleep, and start all over again. We have "experiences." We learn to think that we're powerless—mere pawns to all of life's whims. But we don't realize that "we," as in our higher self, actually have far more power than we believe. We've simply adopted so many constructs or beliefs from the Matrix, from society, that we don't see how fully they control us.

Not long ago, I was going through a difficult time—I was engaged, and then my fiancé and I broke up. I had also been experiencing severe pain in my hip—so much so that it required a replacement. And one of my companies almost went bankrupt. A perfect storm of work, love, and health. It felt like my life was falling apart. I was holding a lot of trauma and pain inside my body, along with many self-limiting beliefs.

I know I'm not alone. I know so many people who seem to have "it all" and yet are struggling physically, mentally, and spiritually. They are in deep psychological pain. As they say, it can be lonely at the top. Feeling powerless can be so lonely and painful—emotionally and to our health. We can all easily slip into periods of pain and desperation. Or we can even begin to see things as a zero-sum game—that if others are happy, successful, thriving, and we're not, it's because they seem to be "taking" what's ours. This is the disastrous mindset known as the "scarcity mindset": the subconscious belief that there is not "enough" in the world.

So how does one shift out of lack and scarcity to feeling enough love, abundance, joy, and all else that is good? By understanding your consciousness. By understanding that your mind has way more power than you think it does. Once you understand this secret, this truth, you can begin to move mountains. That mental pause and reframe is just that hard and yet that simple.

While the pain I was going through was "real" in one sense, it was largely a "construct" of my life and the path I'd been walking down.

Something was unaligned. I hadn't been taking care of myself and working through the traumas of life that were holding me back. I'd had unresolved issues with my father from a young age. I'd been operating in fight-or-flight mode to survive since I was 25 years old. I'd been on stage speaking in front of influential audiences from my early 30s, and I'd been an immigrant with a survivor mindset for as long as I could remember. I'd been hustling and grinding and working myself into the ground, under the false belief (construct) that it was the only way to get ahead. I was also dealing with my own past—Shadow Self, self-imposed limitations, and unconscious beliefs about myself and others. It all came crashing down on me at around the time I turned 45. It was a classic midlife crisis, which I like to reframe as a midlife awakening. I am so grateful the perfect storm came.

Hitting bottom is sometimes the only way to start building your life back up. The universe was clearly showing me that something major in my life was not working.

I took that opportunity to create a new path for myself. I began practicing guided meditations and attending somatic therapy sessions and mindfulness retreats. I also rebuilt my fitness program and nutritional plan. My somatic therapist told me once that our lives are like driving back and forth on an old, muddied road. When we begin to work on ourselves and start seeing and healing our traumas or what's holding us back, we can build a new superhighway right next to the road on which we can find a new personal reality. The old road doesn't go away, but we can choose to take the new one.

If you want to take your life to the next level, truly activate your purpose, and transform your life, you need to understand the power of your mind and its ability to create the universe. Literally. You can change your life one thought at a time.

I'd like to introduce the concept of Horse and Rider that I learned from my friend, Jonathan Hudson. The idea is simply to think of your mind as the rider, and your body as the horse. The question always is, who's in charge? Your mind can control where it goes, when it stops, when it eats, and when it rests. The body, as the horse, must comply. It can only do what the mind tells it to do. However, if you've ever ridden a horse, you know that it takes some practice for the horse to learn how to take the bit, feel the reins, and understand what the rider wants them to do (or not do). It's an intimate relationship. The horse can sense you balking, hesitating, fearing. It can also pick up on your confidence, your ability to communicate, your ability to steer to the final destination. Your body is the same way. If you want to run two miles, but you start off saying to your body, "You can't do this. You suck. You're already in pain. Just give up," what do you think will happen? However, if you tell your body that it's strong, capable, well trained, and excited, how do you think it will respond?

It's also a fact that your body (the horse) has more intelligence than the mind. That's why we are always told to go with our "gut" that's our intuition and our body. Sure, you need the mind to stop from crossing traffic when there are oncoming cars, but the body holds the intelligence. When was the last time you gave your body a voice? Especially one equal to and sometimes greater than your mind? This has been a game changer for me and reminds me that the horse is in charge if I want to get on the right path.

Most of us, however, don't have a hint of our mind's power over our body. We are so unaware of our thoughts, the constructs and beliefs we've come to assume are "facts," that we don't even understand its relationship to the body.

Enter the power of interoception, the ability to sense and interpret internal signals from the body (heartbeat, breath, hunger, temperature, etc.). It can be accessed and honed by doing a body scan in a meditative state from the soles of your feet to the crown of your head.

Interoception is different from identifying your external senses (sight, smell, taste, hearing, and touch). Rather, it involves becoming familiar with the sensations occurring inside the body. Can you feel the muscle twinge in your right calf? Can you hear your heart beating? Are you aware of your right pinky toe or your left thumb? Can you feel your lungs expand when you breathe in? Or the pit in your stomach? If you're able to get still and listen to your body, you will also begin to understand some of your thoughts. Then you'll be able to affect your body through the thoughts you actively choose to think.

This realization literally changed my life. By incorporating somatic tracking (the ability to notice what is going on inside my body in the present moment), I was also able to become aware of some of my thoughts and how they impacted my physical well-being.

I became aware that fear, anger, and sadness literally felt like a contracting force. These emotions were stiffening my back, tightening my hips, and making my neck more tense. But when I felt or imagined more loving kindness, more compassion, and more joy, my body felt light and expansive. I felt my muscles relax, and the tension in my jaw and neck release. Soon, my body began to feel better all over.

---

ACTIVITY

## Plan To Take On the World—But First, Meditate

Back in the late 1970s, Jon Kabat-Zinn, a pioneering mindfulness researcher, founded, developed, and launched the Mindfulness-Based Stress Reduction (MBSR) program—in short, a simple body-scan meditation, and one of my favorite practices. Kabat-Zinn secularized meditations from centuries-old Buddhist teachings to make them more readily accessible to the masses. Body-scan meditations are now used by physicians, psychologists, yoga instructors, meditators, somatic healers, and many more.

Now it's your turn.

The whole purpose of this exercise is to quiet the mind—to dispel all the negative thinking, preconceived notions and stories, projections of the future, ruminations of the past, and focus only on the present, and as a result, calm the central nervous system and thereby the entire body.

1. Get comfortable. You can sit upright in a chair, or on the floor, or lie flat on your back, arms at your sides or draped over your stomach.
2. Close your eyes. I find it helpful to tense up every muscle from toes to head, then contract and squeeze every muscle in my body like a tight fist until I can't anymore. After you do this, let go, and feel the sensation of melting a bit after releasing the tension.
3. Take one long breath through your nose, counting 1, 2, 3, 4 as you inhale, then exhale slowly through your nose while counting 1, 2, 3, 4. Do this three times.
4. Start to feel the weight of your body. Feel all the spots that connect to the earth/ground. Note them.
5. Now imagine roots pulling your body down, deep into mother earth.
6. Let your attention go to any sensation in the body. Start at the soles of your feet. Are your toes tight? How do your shins feel? Your thighs? Working up to your strong back, can we let go a little bit? Does your neck feel tense? Can you loosen it a bit? Is your jaw tight? Can you loosen that too? Is your breathing slow or hurried? Just note it. Don't attach a story to it. (Such as, *I am doing it wrong. If I was*

*doing this right I should have a slow heart rate, etc.*) Let all that go. Just notice.

7. Sit or stay with any unpleasant sensation. Don't try to adjust, move on, or escape. Rather, breathe into the area and send breath to it. If this feels forced, try visualizing the area—picture the muscle relaxing, or the bone healing, or the cells becoming new. Send love, light, or healing energy to the area.
8. Take your time. Once you've noticed all the *obvious* sensations, I want you to go through the body head to toe or reverse. Note your head, inside the head, outside, your forehead, eyes, nose, mouth, throat, and so forth.

You've just taken an important step in becoming embodied and connected with yourself. You can do it yourself or use one of the many apps or videos available that help guide people through body scans. There is no wrong way or right way.

# Part 2

# Take On the World by Going O.H.F. and Working Your Plan

All icons, legends, and greats are doing what I call "going O.H.F." (pronounced "off"):

- They are completely **O**bsessed.
- They are putting in the **H**ours.
- They are 100% **F**ocused.

That is the constant throughline I experience when spending time observing the masters of their craft—the *icons.* And once you know your Purpose, you, too, can go O.H.F.

Do you remember our "fan the flames" activity from part 1? When I tell someone to fan the flames, what I mean is to go absolutely O.H.F. on it. This is without a doubt the formula for success if you want to become like one of your favorite icons or legends, like the PTTOW! members we met in part 1—Quincy Jones, who went O.H.F. on music; Shaun White, who went O.H.F. on snowboarding; Kelly Slater, who went O.H.F. on surfing—and the members we'll meet in part 2. Their common trait isn't just talent, opportunity, or a support system that allowed them to flourish—it's their ability to go O.H.F.!

Paris Hilton went O.H.F. on business, beauty, and wellness (chapter 8).

Diana Nyad went O.H.F. on swimming (chapter 9).

Danny Way went O.H.F. on skateboarding (chapter 14).

Yvon Chouinard, founder of Patagonia, went O.H.F. on saving the planet (chapter 15).

No matter what you plan to go O.H.F. on, in the next chapters we'll learn to expand our vision and dreams, face and conquer our obstacles, master rejections and failure, and ultimately plan for our own success and what comes after.

*My question to you is: What are you obsessed with? What are you willing to commit hours of your life to, with intense focus?*

Are you choosing to put in the work, or are you blowing it off—going to the beach, hitting happy hour with friends, indulging in hobbies, taking long lunches, leaving early, or spending your downtime binge-watching shows—when you know you should be going O.H.F.? Deep down, you always know when you're avoiding your work. Masters of their craft don't let distractions pull them away from their purpose. That's what blackout focus means: refusing to let anything dilute your commitment. I'm not telling you to cut every fun activity out of your life—only to recognize that the icons who achieve greatness stay locked in. They don't let themselves get distracted from the prize of their purpose.

You already know what your version of O.H.F. looks like. Maybe it's obsessing over the brand refresh. Or running scenarios the night before your board meeting to make sure the story lands.

You're not doing it for approval. You're doing it because you *own* what's at stake.

This is the part of the journey where healthy obsession isn't optional. It's what separates those who flirt with greatness from those who *actually* ship it.

Go O.H.F.—not for the headlines, but because this is what mastery demands.

I believe anyone can become successful if they go O.H.F. every day and pursue their purpose with obsession, hours, and blackout focus. If you do so, I have no doubt that within a month you'll begin to see results, within six months your life will begin to change, and by the end of the year I wouldn't be surprised if you, too, had managed to do the impossible.

ACTIVITY

# Plan To Take On the World by Going O.H.F.

## Step 1: Name Your OBSESSION

Many years ago, I knew I had an obsession to launch PTTOW!, but I hadn't yet identified it as such. Once I had named that obsession, I knew I could start doing the work to get it up and running.

What are you obsessed with?

Name it.

A note for those of you who struggle with feeling motivated, let alone obsessed: Get curious. Curiosity will lead you to some unexpected journeys. Just by following your curiosity, you may discover an interest you'll soon want to do day and night. You won't know if you don't try. So try lots of things until you find something you absolutely fall in love with.

I also recommend lowering the stakes. Don't put so much pressure on yourself at first if you don't have something you're obsessed with. Spend some time experimenting, playing, and fanning the flames of your passions.

## Step 2: Commit to the HOURS

Next, you need to eat, breathe, and sleep while thinking about the goal/obsession around the clock. Writing a book? Carry a notebook everywhere. Set a timer to write every day. Tell a friend it's getting published next year and give yourself a deadline for submitting it to publishers. Want to run a marathon or an ultramarathon? Hire a coach, join a running club, or set your alarm for an hour or two earlier every morning to begin training—or, to really commit, sign up for a race. Want to be promoted at work? Make a plan to crush it each day—get there early, stay late. Do whatever is asked, and go above and beyond.

## Step 3: BLACKOUT FOCUS

Tell friends and family you can't make it to your aunt's birthday party. Tell your friends you're not going out for drinks Friday because you have to be up early for a run. Turn off your phone's notifications. Remove distractions. Create a space that is just for you. Hire a coach or an assistant if your budget allows to help you stay focused and accountable to your goals.

Now go crush it.

# Chapter 9

## Name the Impossible Goal

> You tell me what your dreams are. What are you chasing? It's not impossible. Name it.
>
> —Diana Nyad

When I think of a lightning bolt in human form, I think of Diana Nyad.

The first time Nyad stepped off dry land to do the NBDB, she was a young, fit, fearless athlete. In her 1978 memoir, aptly titled *Other Shores*, she wrote about her attempt to swim around Manhattan in autumn 1975. She also spoke about it at our events. She wanted to break the record, but she contracted a virus in the contaminated East River and had to abandon the swim. But she was determined. After 10 days of recovery, she tried a second time. Swimming against the tide and forceful waves, Nyad managed to do the impossible. She swam around the entire island in 7 hours, 57 minutes and broke the record by a full hour.

Even after this mind-boggling achievement, Nyad was unsatisfied. Something deep inside her was pulling on her heart. She knew the most difficult human feat—mentally and physically—was swimming in great bodies of water. And she was someone who felt called to do the most difficult thing.

As a child, her mother would take her to the beach in Ft. Lauderdale, point past the horizon, and say, "You could swim to Cuba, it's so close." Of course, her mom was speaking figuratively; the waters between Florida and Cuba are some of the roughest parts of the ocean. The strait is as wide as five English Channels, with strong, unrelenting currents and rough waves. Last but not least, these waters are filled with sharks and deadly box jellyfish. Unfazed, at 29 years old and in her physical and mental prime, Nyad went for it. Dropping into the water in a shark cage, she began her swim out of Havana Harbor.

Quickly, everything that could go wrong did. The weather turned. Massive waves crashed into her cage, and the Gulf Stream current carried her off course—so much so she unwittingly was swimming toward Texas, not Florida. Nevertheless, she persisted. After nearly 42 hours of swimming and being attacked by jellyfish, ultimately covering 79 miles, she was forced to give up.

Defeated but undeterred, she changed course.

Just one year later, on her 30th birthday, unassisted and without a shark cage, Nyad broke the open-ocean world record for both men and women, swimming 102 miles from the Bahamas to Florida. It wasn't Cuba to Florida, but she felt she was done. Feeling that 30 was a good age for an athlete to retire, she left marathon swimming. She leveraged her love of athleticism into a sports career on television and radio, reporting and commenting for ABC's *Wide World of Sports* and NPR. Nyad also made the rounds as a motivational speaker and writer—even speaking at PTTOW!.

But something happened when Nyad turned 60 that transformed her—her mother died. She realized she wasn't going to live forever either. As most people do when facing their own mortality, Diana knew she had to reckon with all the things she had never done. She asked herself: *Who have you become?* As she told *The New Yorker* in 2014, "Because this one-way street is hurtling toward the end now, and you better be the person you admire." Her mother's passing wasn't just about grief—it was a mirror. Mortality has a way of stripping away excuses, and for Diana it brought back every unfinished dream. She realized she couldn't let her failures at 29 be the last word. At 60, she wasn't just chasing records—she was chasing redemption. She didn't want to wonder what could have been, or dwell on her past failures or fears. Nor did she want to rely on who she once was. "I used to be such a maverick in the nineteen-seventies," she told *The New Yorker*. "I was one of the few people—certainly one of the few women—doing these kinds of extreme things."*

She wondered if she could "rekindle" the dream she had to swim from Cuba to Key West—even in her 60s.

With this new dedication and focus—and understanding of her imminent mortality—she wanted what she called the "thrill of commitment" and a "magnificent goal that would consume all self-doubt."

This time, though, she would do it as she had for the Florida–Bahamas swim: no cage. Her navigation team calculated that the swim would take three to four days. She made an attempt in 2011, but had to stop after about 28 hours in the water, due to an extended asthma attack. The following month she swam for 41 hours but succumbed to venomous box jellyfish stings. She tried again in August

* Daniel Menaker, "Diana Nyad Breaks the Waves," *The New Yorker*, February 10, 2014, https://www.newyorker.com/magazine/2014/02/10/breaking-the-waves.

2012, but once again was forced to stop before reaching Key West due to storms and jellyfish stings.

Most people would have taken these as signs to quit. Diana treated them as learnings, not warnings. Each attempt gave her new data, new strategy, and new resilience. It's the same pattern I've seen again and again in our community: Setbacks become blueprints. They don't close the door—they widen it. Any mere human or superhuman would have thought to stop by then . . . but not Diana.

On Nyad's fifth attempt to swim solo from Cuba to Florida on the morning of August 31, 2013, she hit her stride. She followed a line dragged in the water by a support boat to keep her on course. For part of the journey, she wore a bodysuit, gloves, booties, and a special mask to protect her from jellyfish. In other words, she used her past failed attempts as instructions, not warnings or reasons to give up. However, she did have one major snafu. Her mask caused her to take in a lot of salt water, which made her vomit throughout much of the swim.

She pressed on. She kept her eyes set on the horizon. Her arms pulled her forward. Though weary, and beyond exhausted from swimming for three days, Diana was resolute. She was going to finish. She knew it was her time. And she did it! As she reached the Key West shoreline, the ballooning crowd rushed toward her in the water. Delirious and barely able to stand, she shakily walked toward the shore, more determined than ever to finish what she started over 30 years before. As she hit the shallows and emerged from the water, she ripped her mask off and revealed her face, swollen from jellyfish stings. As the crowd roared, Diana knew she was finished. She did it. Collapsing in her friend's arms, she realized her life's dream had come true. She completed the nearly 111-mile journey from Havana to Key West in less than 53 hours.

When she finally got her footing, she turned to the crowd and managed to tell them, "You're never too old to chase your dream."*

After three days of swimming, on September 2, 2013, 64-year-old Diana Nyad became the first person to swim from Cuba to Florida. Without using a shark cage for protection, she swam in one of the most perilous parts of the ocean, filled with jellyfish and sharks, not only surviving but setting a world record. She had done the impossible.

When Diana spoke about this harrowing journey at PTTOW!, I got chills. Her comeback at 60 reframed what's possible for me. It wasn't just about endurance or even fearlessness—it was about redemption. About refusing to let failure be the closing chapter. It's the same lesson we see in Shaun White's story—after crashing and nearly ending his career, he, too, turned pain into blueprint and came back stronger. Different fields, same truth; courage has no expiration date. For me, Nyad's feat was so much more than facing her fears—I mean, come on. Sharks? Jellyfish? Deadly currents that would sweep most mere mortals to the depths of the sea? Despite her fears, the dangers, she achieved the seemingly impossible.

She—and so many others we've hosted at PTTOW!—is the reason I do what I do: to experience the awe and wonder of what's never been done before—the harrowing, the daunting, the inspirational, the impossible—and then show others what's possible.

I believe doing the impossible is the only way that humanity expands. If we don't do the NBDB, we stand still, which to me is the ultimate failure. If you stand still, you're moving backward. When we

* You can watch her epic arrival onshore after almost 111 miles of swimming at https://www.youtube.com/watch?v=mcvjiw582G0 or you can watch the movie *Nyad*, starring Annette Benning and Jodie Foster, on Netflix at https://www.netflix.com/title/81447231.

as humans set out to do the seemingly impossible, we push the line out farther for what *is* possible. Remember when the four-minute mile was impossible? Remember when flying was impossible? Or motorized vehicles? Yeah. For us to grow as a species, we cannot, as French author André Gide put it, "discover new oceans unless you have the courage to lose sight of the shore." At some point in the Hero's Journey, we have to take that maiden voyage and set off on our own.

If not us, then who? If not now, then when?

On July 21, 1969, the world changed forever when Neil Armstrong stepped off the lunar module to fulfill the mission of Apollo 11 to bring humans to the moon. And when he said, "That's one small step for man, one giant leap for mankind," the world listened in hushed amazement, awe, and wonder.

What the world didn't see is that the moment almost didn't happen.

Moments before, Armstrong, Michael Collins, and Buzz Aldrin had to overcome several challenges and last-second maneuvers. Computer alarms went off, and the astronauts had to call to Mission Control to make sure it was safe to land. The computer was guiding them to a boulder field that would most certainly damage the vehicle and possibly kill all onboard. Instead, Armstrong needed to manually land the module with just 25 seconds of fuel remaining. No one on the ground knew how close to catastrophe these astronauts were. And yet, they landed and walked on the moon, risking their lives so that all of humanity could see more, be more, achieve more.

The astronauts knew it was all so much bigger than the three of them. For they knew what a marvel of human achievement landing on the moon was. Apollo 11 didn't just take a group of men strapped to tons of rocket fuel to get them there—it took millions of individual parts across the entire system, from the Saturn V rocket to the lunar module, all working in perfect harmony. And when I say original parts, I mean *original*. The metals required had yet to be developed! Technologies had to be invented. That is what pushing the boundary does. It led to the greatest human achievement ever. *What does that do?* It completely reframes hope and unlocks what's possible for humanity and in all of our lives. Deep down, the fact that anyone could have done this is a very human story. Take Diana—she was a woman in her 60s, and she did what many athletes in their physical prime never could.

Whenever these big feats happen, most of us don't ponder the details. When men landed on the moon, you saw it in the headlines, but that's not the impressive part. The impressive part is that millions of people joined forces to get those men there within 10 years.

In 1961, when President John F. Kennedy called on Congress and urged them to consider committing "themselves to achieving the goal, before this decade is out, of landing a man on the Moon and returning him safely to Earth," the idea was neither widely approved of nor accepted. In fact, 58% of Americans were not only opposed to the idea but also thought it was frivolous, pointless, and simply couldn't be done. Why waste the money on something that had been impossible up until then?

What those people lacked, but which JFK had, was imagination. Most failures indeed stem from a lack of imagination. Even though JFK would never live to see his dream realized, the world did. We all benefited from this momentous achievement. They did what had never been done in thousands of years of human civilization. That's why I get emotional about it to this day. It's not for the faint of heart.

Because of this daring dream, we all can reach for the moon of our own imaginations. We can all try to do what's impossible, even when others can't see the purpose of our dream. We don't need their approval—we only need our desire. Because in the end, it's our lives, no one else's, at stake. And yes, our lives are at stake.

When Neil Armstrong landed on the moon, his life was at stake, but so was the NASA engineers' entire life work—along with America's reputation. When Diana swam across the Florida Straits, so much was at stake for her—not just her life, but her belief in herself. She set out on that impossible journey to achieve a "magnificent goal" and to eradicate "all self-doubt." She didn't want to live a life of regrets, of never having achieved what she set out to do. No one held a gun on her family and said, "You've got to swim from Cuba, or they all die." And no one forced the USA to send some man to the moon. America did it because we wanted to be the first to push human achievement and human ingenuity.

And that is what I am asking of you: *Can you give your life's work to something that you may think is hard or impossible to achieve, too, and see what is possible? Rather than only reaching for your bedroom ceiling, what if you shot for the stars, missed—and landed on the moon?* How can you dream big, then double that dream and finally double that dream one more time and shoot for that?

When I watch Diana achieve what she did, it fills me with flow. I get giddy about it. Once I'm overflowing with that, I get to share with others, so they, too, experience the awe of human achievement. At PTTOW!, by giving a stage to someone like Diana, we're able to show the world what is possible. To do the NBDB. To have a Plan To Take On the World and then execute it.

My hope is when you are staring down the barrel of your own life and mortality, you think of Diana getting attacked by the lethal sting of box jellyfish, swimming nearly 111 miles in shark-infested waters, pushing her body and mind to the brink of what's possible. I hope you think of a module landing on the moon. I hope it allows you to form a "magnificent goal of your own" and "consume all self-doubt" of your own abilities, follow your own purpose, live life full throttle, and die with no regrets.

Most high performers haven't fully named their "impossible" yet. They're leading teams, scaling companies, sitting in the boardroom—but that next bold move, the one that would stretch them beyond what's already been built? It often stays quiet. Maybe it's launching something new inside the company, building a legacy brand, or taking a swing they've been thinking about for years but haven't said out loud.

That's what Diana did. She didn't start over—she chose to go deeper. She named the goal, owned it, and showed up again and again until it was real. That's what separates those who plateau from those who leave a mark—those who don't just stay afloat, but learn how to swim in deeper waters.

---

ACTIVITY

## Plan To Take On the World by Naming the Impossible

Diana Nyad's journey wasn't just about swimming. It was about conviction. She chased a dream most believed unachievable, and in doing so, redefined possibility. She literally did what was previously thought impossible.

Use this reflection to channel your own bold pursuit.

### Step 1: What are you chasing?

Describe your deepest ambition—not the "should" or the "safe" one, but the wild, aching desire that pulses beneath the surface. The one that scares you a little.

## Step 2: Do you believe you can do it?

Unpack your belief system. What evidence do you have that it's possible? What fears still whisper otherwise?

## Step 3: Declare it.

Because your purpose can't hit a target that you're afraid to name. Take a breath. Center yourself. And finish this sentence:

## It's possible to . . .

Bonus Activity: Write that sentence on a piece of paper and post it on a mirror or other prominent place where you will see it every day.

# Chapter 10

# Work Is Love Made Visible

> And he alone is great who turns the voice of the wind into a song made sweeter by his own loving.
>
> Work is love made visible.
>
> And if you cannot work with love but only with distaste, it is better that you should leave your work and sit at the gate of the temple and take alms of those who work with joy.
>
> —Kahlil Gibran, "On Work"

One of my favorite poems of all time is by the poet Kahlil Gibran. "On Work" perfectly encapsulates what happens to us when we embody our purpose and make it our life's work. He tells us that to work in your purpose is to be love: "Work is love made visible."

For me, our life is about finding this love, this work. When you find your purpose, you're in flow, the hours fly by, and your obsession and focus carry you through. When you're in the zone, you're as close as it gets to pure love and joy. When time stops, that is love. Love is pure unadulterated joy. From love comes joy, and from joy comes happiness, not the reverse. All of this is to say if you want to feel joy, contentment, peace, and happiness, you must love. And what is love? It is work made visible. It is living your purpose—every day—as work.

Working in purpose but just going through the motions, or following every whim and passion with no real commitment, is like the difference between swiping right on a dating app and committing to the work of a long-term relationship. Work is committing to your purpose. In other words, yes, you're going to be in flow, and it's going to be great, but don't dismiss hard work, grit, and perseverance. Gibran writes, "Always you have been told that work is a curse and labor a misfortune. But I say to you that when you work you fulfill a part of earth's furthest dream, assigned to you when the dream was born, And in keeping yourself with labor you are in truth loving life, And to love life through labor is to be intimate with life's inmost secret."

When you work, you are loving life—and you therefore have found the secret to a great life. A life no one else has lived, that no one ever will live.

To have a Plan To Take On the World is to live a life no one else ever has or ever will.

When you are working in love, no matter what you do, you are doing the impossible. You are achieving greatness in your own right. That is SUCCESS. You are coming ALIVE. Do you worry you are not enough? Or are you afraid of digging in and doing the hard work of your purpose? Or worse, do you feel that, because your work is not well known or famous, you don't have a "legitimate" purpose that your love—your work—doesn't matter? What I am here to tell you—what Kahlil Gibran told us all over a hundred years ago—is that no matter if you're a sandal maker or sculptor, your work matters. As Gibran says, "The wind speaks not more sweetly to the giant oaks than to the least of all the blades of grass."

Success is an inside job, not the story society has sold us. That's why we need to find our purpose, the thing that makes us come alive.

Do you daydream about winning the lottery? Inheriting millions? Never having to work again in your life? I hear it a lot as a leader: "I just wish I didn't have to work." I also hear, "I wish this wasn't so hard." But commitment is hard. Love isn't always roses and candlelit dinners. It's showing up when your partner is sick in bed, it's taking the garbage out, it's cleaning the dishes after you cook a meal. It's calling to check in and see if they arrived safely to their destination, even if you're busy. Love is the fruit of all the work you have put into it.

The time you spend working on your purpose, with joy and intention, and without bitterness or wishing to be anywhere else, is what becomes the gold. Trust me, there is always going to be shit to clean up. A mother loves her child even when she is changing his diapers. Just because you have hard days doesn't mean you're not living your purpose. It doesn't mean you need to quit; it might be a sign you need to buckle down and commit. Show up. See the value in what you do and how you're contributing to the greater good and whole. Because when we step into that cosmic procession, we actually become one with everyone and everything.

But even when you are fully in your purpose, there are things in your work you will hate doing. It might be dealing with legal contracts or balance sheets or HR issues—and those are the best-case scenarios.

Yet this is okay. The gold is in doing the disciplined things and getting out of our comfort zone. One of my favorite quotes is from *The Alchemist* by Paulo Coelho: "Every second of the search is an encounter with God, even if you don't achieve the Quest, the Quest itself is the achievement."

Maybe that's why I'm so drawn to the circus. The circus is a metaphor for life—everything, everyone, everywhere happening all at once. Like life. There's laughter, joy, hard work, skill, talents, fear, falls, and drops from great heights. There's rising up again. There's danger, risk, and unknowns. And there's rewards and fun, joy and flow. There's continuous motion and a oneness with everything.

We aren't in the circus; the circus is in us. And when you work your purpose in the flow of the universe, you become part of something completely bigger than yourself. You are the perfection of the universe made visible. You are the WOW you've been looking for.

That idea runs counter to everything we're taught in the West about work. Here, work is a means of survival. We *have to* go to work. Work is something to be despised. A grind. It's something unavoidable we must do until we retire or die. We waste so much precious time and energy, when we could be rejoicing and living in our purpose, our love, our work, our WOW.

---

ACTIVITY

## Making Your Love Visible

The purpose of this activity is for you to begin to do "the work." In the first part of this activity, I invite you to begin to connect the dots between your purpose with tangible expressions of love through reflective writing and purposeful action. Take a few minutes to jot down some responses to these prompts. I know these reflections have helped me rethink my own work from something to be dreaded or something "I had" to do, to something I "get to do." That shift has helped me see what I really do love.

### Step 1: Journal Activity—What Work Means To You

- How was I raised to view "work"?
- Is work a form of survival? Safety?

- Is work something you wish to avoid? Or do you love it? Why?
- In what kind of work do you feel the most "love"? Can you give yourself permission to love your work?
- What are three ways your work, no matter how humble, contributes to others or the greater world?
- What are one to three ways you can bloom where you currently work? What are the things about your job that you love the most and want to do more of?
- What are one to three things you do *not* love and would like to do less of?
- Can you road-map what parts of your work you want to do more of? What parts of your work do you want to do less of over the next six months? One year?
- Describe what "coming alive through work" looks like for you.

## Step 2: Embodied Action—Love in Motion

Within the next 72 hours, take one meaningful action that makes your "love visible through your work." Here are some suggestions:

- Find a project you would love to do and take it to completion.
- Reach out to someone who inspires your purpose.
- Organize your workspace to honor your craft.
- Do a task with intentional joy.

Chapter 11

# Expand Your Vision and Dream Bigger

You cannot swim for new horizons until you have courage to lose sight of the shore.

—William Faulkner

I was never going to be the star athlete, or the smartest kid in the class. I couldn't stand junior high school, and I definitely wasn't one of those kids who thought high school was their peak experience. I was always looking for ways to set myself apart. When kids were studying abroad for college—to Paris and Barcelona—I picked Moscow.

While most of my peers were joining firms and starting their entry-level jobs at 22, I chose to work at Club Med. I didn't want to be a cliché, boring, or like everybody else. But that was interesting, because the six-year-old version of me *did* want to be like everybody else—he wanted a hamburger for lunch instead of the hot beef Stroganoff served at home.

The reality was that if I was comfortable, safe, or the "same" as the crowd, I would never have felt the need to branch out on my own or try things differently. As for most folks, my "initiation" on the Hero's Journey began in school. I set out on my own from there, and I faced the first of many trials and tribulations.

I was an average student and nearly failed English class, so the idea that I have written a book is wildly unexpected (yet another example of getting everything you *didn't* know you wanted). I had no business striving for elite schools, but I was a rule breaker.

When everyone was applying to colleges, I wanted to go to the best. Wasn't that, too, part of the American Dream—going to the "best" school? Or more accurately, it was the dream of my mother, aunts, uncles, and community, who were always talking about success, status, and the importance of getting into a good school, making a lot of money, and driving expensive cars. Through them, I fell into the Matrix and began to want what they wanted for me—material success and notoriety.

I wanted the best of everything, and that included attending a top university like UCLA. I remember I had a wonderful guidance counselor, Mrs. Zabel, who looked at me square in the face and said, "Listen, Roman, not everyone's made for the UC system." It was a kind way of saying: *You're never going to get in. Keep dreaming, Roman. But let's find you a more realistic alternative.*

Life has a way of showing you how to "play small" from the very beginning—usually by well-meaning adults who don't want to see us disappointed. Nevertheless, what she said really landed with me. I knew deep down, even if the world couldn't see it, that I, too, was worthy of the same dream as all of my peers. I, too, wanted to go to

UCLA. And of course, the best way to get me to achieve something, was to tell me I couldn't do it . . .

*There had to be a way.*

And sure enough, there was. In his book, *The Third Door: The Mindset of Success*, my friend Alex Banayan talks about how there are always three ways in. The first door is the front door—the conventional path, where you follow the rules, get the grades, and wait your turn. The second door is the VIP entrance—reserved for those with connections, privilege, or legacy access. But then there's the third door—the one where you find another way in, whether it's through the back door, the side entrance, or even the garbage chute if necessary.

Because of my limitations, I had to figure out workarounds, and I became very adept at finding the elusive third door. I graduated from high school, then enrolled at Cal State Fullerton for a bit before realizing that UC system schools, including UCLA, rarely accept candidates from other four-year colleges, including the Cal State system. However, they did accept many candidates from two-year junior colleges, since after two years, those students would have nowhere to continue college. So I dropped out and started taking courses at Saddleback Community College, where I could eventually transfer into UCLA after two semesters. And that's exactly what I did. I made it through the Third Door.

However, I soon realized I hated college. Community college, state, and even the elusive and prestigious UCLA—they weren't for me. Classes were boring, especially ones in my major, economics. Eventually, I found a fraternity I enjoyed and did some social chairing, but I couldn't wait to get out and start the next adventure—adulthood.

At the end of the day, I knew I was there to get a diploma and then just get on with life. Again, that feeling of "not belonging" chased me. Even though I'd gotten to where I wanted to go, I still had a pervasive sense that all of "this" was not for me. It was indeed a "dream," but I wasn't entirely sure it was my dream.

And so again, I moved on. I thought the answer was in the working world. I was obsessed with Wall Street and determined to make it in one of the top six investment banks—also called "bulge-bracket" firms. There were 60 spots for some 6,000 applicants, so I immediately started looking for the third door. I applied to 72 investment banks, many much worse than those in the movies *Wolf of Wall Street* or *Boiler Room*—literally, they would have been in the top 30—and out of 72 applications, I got 73 rejection letters (JPMorgan rejected me *twice*).

A bulge-bracket bank position was one of the hardest, most prestigious, and highest-paying jobs to land coming out of college in 1997. It was harder to get a job at one of these top six investment banks than it was to get into Harvard. I thought if they just hired me, then I would finally receive the feeling of ultimate acceptance . . . that if I could just make it on Wall Street, then everyone would see I belonged. Then I wouldn't just be average Roman, I'd be magnetic. Women would like me, men would want to be around me, and I'd have status. But how did I, Roman, know about this? I had Russian immigrants for parents; it's not as though they had been pushing this dream of Wall Street on me.

Yet as all Hero's Journey goers know, mentors and guides come in all shapes and sizes. I had a friend in Orange County, Paul, who lived in a gorgeous home by the water—his father read the *Wall Street Journal* every day, drove the best cars, and ate at the finest restaurants (and not the Carl's Jr. variety), so I looked up to him. I thought if I could become like him, I'd have it made. Everyone would like me. Everyone would want me at their parties. Best of all, I thought all of my fears would be assuaged, if I slayed the mighty dragon that was Wall Street.

Fear was also driving my pursuit of Wall Street. I had three huge fears:

1. The fear of failure/financial insecurity
2. The fear of loss of status
3. The fear of being perceived as shady and not having integrity

These were, at the heart of it, all things my dad lived and died through. Up until the age of 20, my dad was a present figure and a good force in my life. But when it came to business, his ideas and ventures rarely succeeded, and he lost all his money. It was important to him to be the "big man on campus," but he wasn't, and he was always chasing some outlandish business idea with questionable characters. Much of my childhood had been in the shadow of him trying but failing to find his business footing. It wasn't until I saw how my friends lived, how their dads behaved and worked, that my horizons broadened. They depicted an alternate reality for what could be possible in my own life.

Of course, when I was young, I didn't realize my fears were driving so many of my behaviors and choices—or that once I got to the heart of those fears, I'd see what I really longed for.

---

ACTIVITY

## Sebastian Terry's Four Steps to Creating Your "100 Things to Do Before You Die" List

One of my dear friends and members of PTTOW! is Sebastian Terry, author of *100 Things: What's On Your List?* He has commanded the PTTOW! stage for us and has a wonderful exercise for considering your own mortality and doing the NBDB. He believes it's not until we face our own mortality that we can get real about what we want to achieve in this life. He leads breakout groups through an exclusive eight-step process to examine one's own life and set goals for themselves. And he should know; after facing his own mortality, he assembled a list of 100 things he wanted to do before he died and *he has done most of them.*

This exercise will walk you through the first four of the eight steps to get your wheels turning and create your list.

**Step one is permission.** Just give yourself permission to think about yourself. It's not selfish, it's not negative—it's really selfless, ultimately, because it makes you a better person for other people.

**Step two is to reflect on your life.** You can't change what's happened beforehand, but reflection allows us to understand not only what we value in life but also how we've shown up in our lives thus far. It might be helpful to write a eulogy and highlight things about yourself. How have we shown up as a person? Have we chased our biggest dreams? Do we have regrets? Have we been our most authentic selves?

**Step three is to consider the spokes to your wheel of life.** Imagine a wheel with spokes. Now imagine that wheel is your life. What are the spokes that make your life stronger? It could be anything, but typically it's family, connection, adventure, education, and maybe spirituality. There could be a million things. But if you're able to identify those spokes on your wheel of life, you can use them as the foundation to begin building meaningful goals to better strengthen your life.

**Step four is creating a list.** So, what are your 100 things? What are the goals, dreams, and aspirations that would go on to strengthen each of your spokes? The goals don't have to be world changing (although they can be!); they just have to be personally meaningful.

# Chapter 12

## Face and Conquer Obstacles

> Just do what's necessary, then do what's possible. And before you know it, you're doing the impossible.
>
> —Francis of Assisi

When Janine Shepherd was a young Olympics-bound skier, she taught herself a skill while training that would one day save her life: She learned to love the hills. Not only did they make her physically strong; they also made her mentally tough. And because they were difficult, no one else loved them, which, Janine says, gave her an edge. But the main thing the hills taught her was that just when you think you've conquered one, there's another . . . and another . . . and another.

By accepting this reality, she knew she could be unstoppable. While others were prepared to just coast, she knew to keep pedaling, taking one hill at a time—even the most devastating and life altering of hills.

This skill would come in handy. One day in 1986 while training with her Australian ski team for the 1988 Winter Olympics, her life changed in an instant on a hill. One minute she was riding her bike from Sydney to the Blue Mountains with her ski team; the next she was being airlifted away after being hit by a speeding utility truck.

Janine wasn't expected to make it. She had broken her neck, back (in six places), five ribs on her left side, right arm, collarbone, and several bones in her feet. Her entire right side was ripped open and filled with gravel, and her head was cut open, exposing the skull. The extensive head and internal injuries caused massive blood loss. By the time the helicopter got her to a Sydney hospital, Janine says, "My blood pressure was 40 over nothing."*

When Janine joined us at our 2014 PTTOW! summit, she explained that she didn't remember the accident, because she had already left her body. For the next 10 days, she drifted between two worlds. One part of her was in intensive care in excruciating pain, and the other part was looking on from above. She didn't want to go back to her broken body, but she finally made the decision to return, and her internal bleeding suddenly stopped. However, when she woke, the doctor told her she had a bone stuck in her spine that needed to be removed in what is called an anterior decompression laminectomy. They literally cut her spine in half in order to pick all the fragments out of her spinal cord. The doctors were excited because they believed the operation was a success, as they had removed the bone, and she had small movement in her toe. However, Janine was ultimately told

---

* Ryan Bergeron, "Olympic Hopeful Re-Imagines Her Life," *CNN*, September 15, 2016, https://www.cnn.com/2016/09/15/health/turning-points-janine-shepherd/index.html.

there "was no cure," and she would be a paraplegic. She could expect no feeling from the waist down and would have to use a catheter for the rest of her life. The doctor said, "Janine, you're going to have to rethink your life because you are never going to be able to do the things you did before."

Having learned from the hills not to accept what was in front of her, Janine refused to accept the life sentence. What she did accept was that she couldn't walk in this moment, but this didn't mean she never would. This distinction—between resignation and true acceptance—became her turning point.

Janine was moved from intensive care to acute spinal care, where she spent the next six months of her life flat on her back: wrapped in a plaster cast, neck braced, head stabilized with sandbags, unable to move her legs. She spent her time in that ward with five other people. Nobody could see each other, because they were all lying flat and looking up at the ceiling. Unlike her, they weren't athletes, and she didn't think she had anything in common with the other patients.

But one night, a nurse entered the ward and put a big pack of plastic straws on each of them. He asked them to start threading the straws together until they all were joined. Because the beds in the spinal ward were positioned in a circle, when they were finished, a large ring of straws wrapped around the spinal ward. It was an incredible moment for Janine. She realized they were all connected, and her life mattered. That circle of straws became her first sign that rock bottom could also be a place to begin again.

In that moment, she wondered, "If I couldn't ski, then what would I do? How could I contribute to the world after I left the hospital?" She knew she had made a choice to come back to her body, and she was on a quest to know why. What had remained unfinished? She understood she had to accept this new fate, realizing, "Maybe rock bottom is actually the perfect place to start?"

Though she had never thought of herself as a creative person before her accident, she knew she was about to embark on the most creative project ever—rebuilding her life, one step, one hill at a time. She had absolutely no idea what she was going to do. But in that uncertainty came a sense of freedom, because she was no longer tied to a fixed path. That realization changed her life.

Sitting outside in her wheelchair, an airplane flew over her house. She looked up and thought, *If I can't walk, then I might as well fly!* She told her mom that she wanted to learn. Weeks later, her mother and a friend drove her to Bankstown Airport in greater Sydney and carried her into the flying school.

Janine had to be lifted into the cockpit, but once she was there, she felt the most incredible sense of freedom. As they flew over the training area, her friend pointed to the spots where her journey had begun six months earlier: the mountains where the accident took place and then the ICU where she was taken. Instead of defeating her, the flight exhilarated her. She found a new sense of purpose and resolve. She was going to get her pilot's license—and she was going to do everything in her power to walk again. She started practicing walking as much as she could. She started with two people holding her up, then she used the furniture and walls, then graduated to walking on her own.

With that resolve to fly, she went to her local airfield to learn. Upon announcing that she wanted to fly, the instructor asked how she planned on doing that without the use of her legs. In true Janine form, she said, "Well, I still have two arms and we can figure the rest out." She indeed learned to fly, and earned a rising number of qualifications to fly heavier planes, unrestricted and in bad weather, eventually winning her commercial pilot's license and an instructor rating. And she still wasn't done. She went back to school to learn how to teach people how to fly, and then—yes, there's more—how to fly acrobatically and then teach that. She did this all within 18 months after building a circle with straws in the spinal ward!

Although she knew for certain her body would never be that of an Olympian, she had the spirit of one. And that is what made her unstoppable.

When she talked to PTTOW!, she shared a technique that helped her get through those difficult early days. "When I used to cycle, I never looked at the top. I looked down at the ground and I watched my feet step by step until eventually I was at the top of the hill. Francis of Assisi says it so simply: 'Just do what's necessary, then do what's possible. And before you know it, you're doing the impossible.'" Her lesson: You don't leap to the impossible—you walk there, one small step at a time.

The only thing she could do when she got home after her accident was to accept her situation. But acceptance is not resignation. Acceptance is empowerment. Acceptance, Janine said, was simply stating what has happened and that it was in the past. Once you do that, you can ask: "Now what?" She answered, "All you have to do is take the next step." Before she knew it, she was doing the impossible. She wasn't just meant to live. She wasn't just meant to walk. She was meant to fly. She was meant to do the things that everyone else says is impossible.

"I now know that there is no problem too difficult that it can't be solved, or any hill too steep that it can't be climbed," Janine said. "And the only thing that life requires from us is to be completely and fully in this moment right here where you are because there is no other moment. This is it."

When Janine Shepherd came to PTTOW!, she didn't just walk. She cartwheeled. I am not exaggerating; she literally was doing cartwheels and front somersaults on the stage at our party. That's the image of Janine that comes to me. I see her doing what others thought impossible, and I am so inspired. But what I am most moved by is that Janine's story exemplifies something I truly believe is fundamental when setting out to find your purpose. To do so, you have to hit the lowest valley—some call it rock bottom, some call it a breaking point. No matter what you call it, the valley is sometimes a required destination before stepping into your true purpose. Janine would never have discovered flying if she hadn't been hit by a truck. And it's how she responded to that accident that was so transformational. Instead of being angry, bitter, or throwing up her hands and saying, "Forget it! I give up!" Janine accepted what she couldn't do and opened herself up to new possibilities.

What I love about stories like Janine's is that it makes me—us—feel less alone. We have all been there, in our own way—we've all experienced a moment in our life when a dream we thought was ours was snatched from us. But sometimes we need to have one dream die to reveal our true purpose. That's the paradox of purpose: Sometimes the end of one dream is the beginning of the real one.

---

ACTIVITY

## Plan To Take On the World One Hill at a Time

When you set out on your journey, you inevitably will meet obstacles. As Janine's story shows us, all we need to do is take one hill at time. Let's break down the process of facing and conquering any obstacle. Pull out your notebook and answer these questions.

## Step 1: Identify Your Hill

- What hill are you facing in your life today—personally, professionally, emotionally, or spiritually?
- Is this hill external (a specific challenge) or internal (a limiting belief)?
- What does this hill look like symbolically? Name it: *The Hill of Fear*, *Mount Uncertainty*, or *The Ridge of Reinvention*.
- Sometimes there is a benefit in visualizing your hill. What does the summit look like? Where are you standing? What is the path or footholds you can grab on to? Draw a picture of what the hill looks like.

## Step 2: Disrupt the Comfort Zone

- Let's try to understand your mindset. What keeps you at the base of the hill? Is it comfort, doubt, or lack of clarity?
- If you took one leap outside your comfort zone today, what would it look like?
- Imagine yourself stepping into uncertainty—not with dread, but with curiosity. Write down the two or three things you are curious about.
- Commit to one small action this week that edges you out of routine—something that makes your heartbeat quicken but feels true to your path.

## Step 3: Loving the Climb

- What if you could love this hill—not just survive it?
- How might reframing this struggle as a gift, teacher, or sacred terrain transform your experience?

- When have you grown most in past ascents?
- Write a short letter to your future self at the summit. Describe what they've learned and how they feel looking back. What was the most challenging part of the journey? What are you most proud of? How do you feel?

*Most of this story was told during Janine Shepherd's talk at PTTOW! 2014, which you can watch at* https://www.youtube.com/watch?vhgiXLFH2wqM. *Or you can read her book,* Defiant: A Broken Body Is Not a Broken Person.

## Chapter 13

# Master Rejection and Failure

> Ever tried. Ever failed. No matter. Try again. Fail again. Fail better.
>
> —Samuel Beckett

While I was getting rejected from every financial firm, I filled a binder with the rejection letters. Instead of feeling defeated by each rejection, I was happy. I felt seen. I felt like a "no" was just one step closer to a yes. Eventually, I started calling firms. I'd say, "Hey, I'm going to be in New York. Can I meet with you?" Two of them said yes, both bulge-bracket firms: Credit Suisse and JPMorgan.

I let each failure teach me. Eventually, I asked, *How can I differentiate myself?* I realized the front door wasn't gonna work. I looked at what did work for me: I could speak Russian. I also recognized I needed to boost my GPA, because I was a C student. I decided to make Russian a minor and began competing against kids who'd never spoken a word of Russian before. Of course, I earned an A. (Life hack alert: Lean into your strengths to give yourself a boost.) I took a study-abroad program in Moscow, which had a developing-capital-markets economy. There were only two of us out of a school of 40,000 going, so I knew I could stand out. I was able to get meetings with major banks like Morgan Stanley, Credit Suisse, and First Boston. When it was time to return, Credit Suisse flew my broke butt back to New York for an interview. When they called to tell me I was hired, I fell to the ground. I couldn't believe it, but I had made it. I thought I had fulfilled my "dream."

At Credit Suisse, I went through an intensive three-month training program. I kept hearing about "Global Power Group," which sounded really exciting to me. I literally thought it was world domination. Who wouldn't want to be in the room with someone from the Global Power Group? I didn't know what they did, but it sounded amazing—until I realized it was a "power" group—meaning natural gas and electricity! You have to learn to laugh at yourself if nothing else! Needless to say, the Global Power Group was not as sexy as what I had expected it to be.

Once my time at Credit Suisse became real work instead of training, reality set in. I knew this wasn't for me. My peers were quant jocks, the kinds of people for whom this was the right job. I couldn't compete. Most importantly, I realized I didn't have passion for it, and without this passion, I wouldn't succeed.

Life is never a straight line. It's a zigzag, a circle, peaks and valleys. Our passions can change too. I used to sit in my dorm room with the impossible dream of working on Wall Street. And not only did I achieve it, but I actually joined a bulge-bracket firm. My passion clearly was there, until I actually did it, and then I realized it wasn't for me. Along the way, I found out that real estate, private equity, and venture capital weren't for me either. After Wall Street, I kept looking and trying for a match to my passions, all the while moving toward entertainment. I thank God all the time for all the rejections (and self-rejections, when I decided things were not for me). If it wasn't for the rejections and setbacks, I wouldn't have had the motivation to be able to achieve something, to find out what I was truly made for.

I also realize now what I didn't see back then—if you have to force something, it's probably not right for you. There is an old saying to be careful what you wish for because you just might get it. I forced matters at times. And once I got them, I was miserable. I wasn't in flow. I found flow going after the audacious goal, but not the experience itself.

If there's one quote that I live by, it's Winston Churchill's: "Success is going from failure to failure without losing enthusiasm." For me, success isn't always in the "Yes." It's in the "No" too. Because the Nos help guide you to where you are meant to be. As long as you don't lose enthusiasm and can keep "cartwheeling" through life as Janine does, the right doors will eventually open for you. And little by little, if you continue moving, you will move closer to where your heart is aligned with your purpose and passion.

---

ACTIVITY

## Rejection Is Redirection

Rejection isn't the end of the road—it's often the nudge toward a path more aligned with who we're becoming. Reflect upon times you felt like a failure or faced rejection. Don't beat yourself up. Instead, try to see how it taught you valuable lessons, led you to force yourself into things, or put you on a path that was meant for you. Ultimately, the purpose of this activity is to help you reframe your rejection and see it in a new light.

## Step 1: Mapping the Misaligned

*"What did I try to force?"*

- Recall a time when you poured energy into something—a relationship, a job, a dream—that just wouldn't take root.
- What signs did you ignore, hoping it might still grow?
- In hindsight, why wasn't it meant for you? What values or truths of yours did it clash with?

## Step 2: What It Revealed

*"What did the 'no' teach me?"*

- What lesson did you learn from this?
- What, if any, recurring patterns did you uncover? Habits of pushing too hard, being influenced by others, chasing for the wrong reasons?
- How did getting rejected sharpen your sense of purpose, if at all?
- Can you see how that NO was maybe one of the best things that happened to you?

## Step 3: Reframing the Rejection

*"Was that a redirection?"*

- Choose one painful rejection. Now, write about it from a future perspective—as a plot twist that led you to growth, healing, or revelation.
- What opportunity emerged because of that door closing?
- If you could thank that rejection, what would you say? Write a short thank-you letter.

# Chapter 14

## Take the Leap of Faith

> Preparation can only take you so far; after that you've got to take a few leaps of faith.
>
> —Michael Scofield

The crowd below was waiting with bated breath. Thousands had gathered at the base of the largest mega-ramp ever constructed. But this wasn't any ramp. This was a ramp constructed specifically for a skateboarder to hurl himself over the Great Wall of China.

Thirty-one-year-old champion skateboarder Danny Way was standing on the precipice, holding his board, staring out over the grand expanse and the two hundred feet below him. Not only did he have to ride down this giant ramp; he also had to launch himself over the Great Wall and land on a ramp on the other side. If he could ride the ramp and the wall, he'd set world records for being the first person to jump the wall and clear 70 feet with a skateboard.

The feat would break cost records too. Danny's sponsor, DC Shoes, had spent $1.5 million just to build the custom ramp.

It was also unprecedented in that this skateboarding event would be telecast—worldwide—to more than 100 million viewers.

The stakes couldn't have been higher for Danny.

And not just because of the cost, the height, or the viewership.

His life was on the line.

During his practice jump the day before, Danny "wobbled and crashed." In lay terms, when he and his board launched from the ramp, he lost his footing and air-kicked himself over to the other side of the wall—barely landing on the ramp in time and therefore escaping what would have been certain death from the fatal height and impact. Thankfully, he made it to the ramp and didn't plunge to his death in front of thousands of people. But he landed hard, crashed, rolled down, and, in the process, broke his ankle. It was soul crushing to the fans below. But Danny was determined. Despite his rattled nerves, he decided he was ready to go through with the jump, broken ankle or not.

The next day, Danny took the long, lonely climb up the stairs with his freshly broken ankle to the top the ramp. He stood for a moment, inhaling and exhaling, taking in the entire scene. That day was also super windy. And there were locusts in the air. The moment was biblical—wind, insects, fear, and one man staring down the impossible.

The crowd looked up, worried. There was a very real possibility that they could be witnessing a death in a few seconds. Danny blocked out all the fear—all of theirs, all of his. Fear, he knew, would either paralyze him or drive him. And he chose drive.

As Danny had said himself many times over, when he and the board are together, they are one. He had been skating since as long as he could remember. This was what he was meant to do. There was no turning back. No other option. No walking back down. It was time to make the leap.

Danny dropped in from 65 feet—the height of a six-story building—and accelerated faster than a Ferrari, cresting 60 mph in seconds. He then launched into the air—up, up, up hitting the record-setting 70 feet—before landing perfectly on the other side.

The crowd went wild. Danny had stuck it and wrote his name in the history books for all time. He'd made a Plan To Take On the World and achieved the NBDB.

But was Danny done? Nope. He had three more runs in him.

Now it was just for fun.

No one would have blamed Danny that day if he'd said, "Nah, this is crazy. I'm out." A mountain biker had died trying the same jump a few years before. But those close to Danny knew something the rest of us didn't—Danny had faith in himself, in the board, in his process. He *knew* he could do it. He wasn't taking some uncalculated risk.

When he failed to make the jump on his practice run, he gathered new intelligence: His drop-in wasn't high enough. So he had them build it a couple feet higher. Danny knew this was about physics as much as it was talent and skill. He needed to hit the right speed to make it across the Wall.

He didn't let the failure shake him. He didn't let it determine who he was or what he could do. He saw it as simply something to learn from and move on. That's the difference between spectacle and mastery: He wasn't gambling, he was calculating.

Doing the impossible usually follows a lot of hard work, practice, time, effort, and yes, failures and mistakes—even public ones.

When I was interviewing Danny with my cofounder Jim for his PTTOW! Icon award, we nearly fell down when he recounted his story. We were blown away that he'd decided to jump after fracturing his ankle. We asked, "Danny, your sponsors, the Chinese government, and the media would have totally understood that you fractured your foot—the one you had to skate on—and couldn't do the jump. Why didn't you just call it a day?"

Danny, being Danny, responded dryly, "You wouldn't be here giving me the Icon award."

He then got serious, "Fear is your friend. You need fear to focus you and prepare you."

I love how Danny has developed a positive relationship with fear. As someone who is afraid of heights, I find the idea that we need to harness fear to achieve our dreams inspiring, yet daunting—but we do. That's a large part of what lets GOATs like Danny Way operate at that level they do: They see fear differently. They don't erase it. They embrace it. And we can't PTTOW! if we don't take that first step. If our fears get the best of us, the naysayers hold us back, or our self-belief wanes, we'll stumble when it's time to leap. Danny's leap reminds us that courage isn't the absence of fear—it's skating straight into it and flying over the wall anyway.

Diana swam toward the horizon when most would have turned back. Shaun faced the halfpipe that almost killed him. Janine traded her skis for wings. Fear takes many forms, but the leap—the choice to keep going—is universal.

> Faith is taking the first step even when you don't see the whole staircase.
>
> —Martin Luther King Jr.

Danny's story reminded me of a chart that has always held space in my mind. It simplifies what it means to achieve nearly any goal—especially the greatest goals. You can stay in your comfort zone and live in a small world, but staying in place is really the same as moving backward, because the world around you is always moving forward.

That wall between you and your dream? Some people call it *pain*. I call it *resistance*. And you can't avoid it—you can only go through it. On the other side of that wall lie endless possibilities.

Think about it:

- If you want to run a marathon, you can't get there without sore muscles, early mornings, and miles of training.
- If you want to grow a business, you can't avoid the setbacks, rejections, and sleepless nights that build resilience.
- If you want to build a world-class team, you can't skip the hard conversations, the missteps, and the vulnerability it takes to lead.

This is what Danny embodies: moving forward through challenge, rather than avoiding it. It's what allows people to do the Never Been Done Before. The chart makes it clear—there's no standing still. You're either moving forward through challenge toward endless possibilities, or you're moving backward into smaller worlds.

---

ACTIVITY

## Plan To Take On the World by Facing Your Fears

You've built. You've led. You've earned the right to coast. But something in you is still restless. That next move, the bold one that could redefine what you're known for? It's standing right in front of you. Danny Way didn't become legendary by playing it safe. He made the leap, fully committed. If fear is the only thing keeping you from going, it's probably the thing you need to do next.

## Step 1: Naming Your Wall

- What challenge feels intimidating, complex, or emotionally turbulent?
- Describe it—not just literally, but metaphorically. Is it jagged, slick, towering, ancient?
- Is your fear rooted in past pain, perceived inadequacy, or future unknowns?

## Step 2: Respecting the Fear

- Zoom in on the sharpest part of the fear. What makes it so terrifying?
- What stories have you told yourself about why you can't or shouldn't leap?
- Who or what reinforces those stories?

## Step 3: Flipping the Frame

- Picture the moment after the leap. What's changed? What doors opened?
- How would success reshape your beliefs or identity?
- What ripple effect might this leap have on others?

## Step 4: The Undeniable Edge

- List your skills, experiences, or insights that position you for this challenge.
- What scars, trials, or quirks sharpen your edge?

- If you believed these traits were gifts instead of gaps, how would you move differently?
- What would happen if it worked out?
- What makes you uniquely skilled or qualified to do it?
- Finish this sentence: *"I leap not because I'm unafraid, but because I'm ________."*

# Chapter 15

# Achieve Success and Plan for What Comes After

> Satisfaction lies in the effort, not in the attainment, full effort is full victory.
>
> —Mahatma Gandhi

I recently went for a hike in Beverly Hills while I was staying at a friend's family's home. I was preparing for a speech and looking for some inspiration, and thought a beautiful view might be just the thing I needed.

I set out excited to get to the peak. I couldn't wait. I was so excited, in fact, I barely stopped along the way to take in the views that were right in front of me. As soon as I reached the summit—sweating and exhausted from the effort—I looked down, and what did I see? A gorgeous vista? A beautiful view?

No, a steaming pile of dog shit. I kid you not.

I had to laugh at myself—at the universe. It was one of those cosmic jokes. So what if you reach the impossible, the summit? What if, on the way, you missed out on all that was happening around you—the life you were meant to see and experience? What does it all mean? Why even do it if all that awaits you is a pile of shit, a steep cliff, or, yes, another mountain? What if you get there and find out you didn't even enjoy the trip? What if you were living for the destination?

How many of us have seemingly "made it" in life, only to feel hollow inside and long for something more? How many of us have followed all the rules—school, college, good job, good pay, vacations, houses, cars—and still feel like something is missing? What does it all add up to? What does it all matter?

When I was working on Wall Street, I thought I'd "made it" to the big leagues. It was everything I thought being successful was. After all, I had grown up wanting and working tirelessly for just this experience. I had done everything in my power to achieve this seemingly impossible dream, only to find out when I got there, the dream didn't align with the reality.

Sure, I liked the obvious benefits—good salary, comfortable lifestyle, vacations, and nice cars. But I didn't love *me*. I didn't love how I felt. The effort wasn't worth the "peak" or summit if it claimed my heart and soul. And it's important to note that at the same time, I'm still grateful and feel lucky that I pursued this dream and lived in the reality—no regrets at all. But I did know at the time that what got me *here* wasn't what was going to get me *there*. Still, I learned so much that would prepare me for what was next—not the least of which, at the age of 22 how to read financial statements and interact with Fortune 500 CEOs and CFOs. These skills would later help me create business plans, P&L statements, and so much more. Most important, I learned when it was time to move on.

Most of us are operating in and living out someone else's dream for us. Or we assume that to be truly "successful," we have to "make it." Most of us think the opposite of success is failure. However, every successful person I know fails and fails a lot. So that begs the question: What is true success? What does it mean to be successful? What have you come to believe success means for you? Do you consider yourself a success or a failure? Have you given any thought to who or what set those standards in the first place? And how do you know that the mountain you are climbing is even the right one for you?

There isn't one of us out there who doesn't know the feeling of working toward some goal or summit, only to reach it and find a steep cliff below us—and beyond that, another mountain to climb. Think of the early pioneers traversing the US with their eyes set on what is now California. Can you imagine how they must have felt when they made it to the eastern edge of the Grand Canyon? Can you imagine traveling all that way, and then looking out across the abyss, knowing you had so many more miles to go, only to find out when you got to the other side, that an enormous desert lay before you, and then more hills and mountains before reaching the coast?

That is what it feels like to be alive. We set out on a journey, thinking we're going one place, only to find out when we get there that our journey is not over. More deserts, mountains, and oceans await.

In the bestselling book *The Second Mountain*, former *New York Times* op/ed columnist David Brooks argues that most people fall into this story that "society" creates for them of what comprises "success" atop the first mountain they encounter. They go to school, start their career, and begin to climb the mountain they think they were "meant to climb." They achieve the C-suite status and bank accounts, able to buy the house, car, lifestyle, and more. Usually this mountain is made of goals that our society, churches, schools, or parents project on us and endorse, often in unnoticeable and loving ways. But when they reach the peak, they look around and realize: *This wasn't my mountain to climb—something feels empty. There is another, steeper, more impossible mountain just out beyond me—and* that, that *is my mountain! One I can bring my whole self to.* Don't get me wrong—in my case, climbing the first mountain was great and a huge deal. I realize that many people never even make it to that first peak, which is simply the prologue for what's next.

So what is that Second Mountain?

According to Brooks, the mountain that is meant for you is one that moves you from being self-centered to other-centered. But I don't agree with this. This philosophy seems to carry an inherent moral judgment—that one must move on from being self-centered to other-centered. Rather, I believe you have to be self-centered first. You have to learn to honor yourself—to put your oxygen mask on first, as Sebastian Terry likes to say—before you are capable of genuinely serving others.

However, I do agree with Brooks in that there is no way you can make it alone. He contends that you need to commit to the path—and to other people. In *The Second Mountain*, Brooks identifies four commitments that define a life of meaning: to spouse/family, a vocation (a calling—your purpose), a philosophy (some people call this a faith), and a community. In fact, our happiness and sense of fulfillment—true success—depends on this.* A further point he makes is how important your vocation/job is as an essential place to find purpose and community. Many of us have found some of our best friends and relationships through work. Work can often be such an important support system for some of our most challenging moments in life as

---

* David Brooks, *The Second Mountain: The Quest for a Moral Life* (Random House, 2019).

well as some of our greatest accomplishments. Fanning the flames of purpose in your workplace can often accelerate your trajectory.

This is not to say that the first mountain should be avoided. That, too, is a tragic error. We all need to experience as many different opportunities as life can present to us. It's how we come to understand the world and see what's for us and what isn't. Had I not tried to make it on Wall Street, it could have been very easy for me to spend the rest of my life regretting that I didn't go for it—or worse yet, resenting myself and others for not seeing my "dream come true." And I learned so many great lessons. Had I not also lost my business, I would not have acquired the wisdom that helped me in my current position as the CEO and cofounder of PTTOW! There are no mistakes or regrets with the past. Just lessons. Life doesn't happen *to us*. It happens *for us*. Everything in the past is a gift. The past is just the prologue for what is next.

We are not victims of what happens to us. Rather, we are empowered, sovereign over our lives. And we must step out of the victim consciousness, which is always a recipe for failure.

Yet there are so many people who live lives of regret, who spend their lives bemoaning their fates—they sound like the late Marlon Brando crying out into the ether, "I could have been a contender!" But what if they could have? Did they take it all the way and actually find out? It's so much easier to be a Monday morning quarterback and look back on your own and others' lives, judging what could have been better. But if you try something and it doesn't work out or resonate, then you definitely know it's not for you. You could also find that it is. For me, Wall Street wasn't it. Nor was my first company it . . . but they were key stepping stones.

Our dreams can and will naturally evolve over time. Take PTTOW! Icon Yvon Chouinard, founder of Patagonia. When Yvon started out, he was literally climbing mountains in a falconry group he had joined, ascending and descending mountains in California to get better views of the birds. When home, he taught himself blacksmithing to create pitons to hammer into the sides of rock to assist with his and his friends' climbing. Soon he began selling the pitons.

After some time, he received complaints that these pitons were defacing the natural beauty of the rock faces he was climbing, so he began looking for alternatives. Eventually he created what he called "chocks" that could be hammered into rock crevices, then removed. This served both his customer base and nature. It was an early clue to the pattern of his life: business as a tool not just to serve him and others, but to serve the planet.

Over time, Yvon's business expanded. Driven by his love of the outdoors, his natural affinity toward climbing, and his desire to share it with his friends, Patagonia was born. During the next 50 years, the company grew—expanding beyond climbing equipment into climbing gear and apparel. You would be hard pressed to set out on a hike and not run into a hiker wearing a Patagonia pullover.

Yvon Chouinard eventually became a billionaire—his company is one of the most successful private companies in the world. You would think he would retire, take his billions, and live his final days out in peace on some island. No one would blame him. Many others have done the same. But Yvon wasn't done. He had a bigger mountain he wanted to climb—more than being a successful entrepreneur. He was ready for his Second Mountain.

In September 2022, Chouinard sent shockwaves through the bedrock of the business community when he released a statement titled, "Earth Is Now Our Only Shareholder." He transferred all of his holdings and profits into the Patagonia Purpose Trust and Holdfast Collective, promising that every dollar not invested into the company itself would be "distributed as dividends to protect the planet." He said, "Instead of extracting value from nature and transforming it into wealth, we are using the wealth Patagonia creates to protect the source. I am dead serious about saving this planet."*

In an open letter on Patagonia's website, Chouinard stated, "I never wanted to be a businessman. I started as a craftsman, making climbing gear for my friends and myself, then got into apparel."†

In other words, Chouinard started a company to *serve himself* and his friends. It was a small venture he started in a tin shed. It was never intended to be the global powerhouse it is today. But something shifted inside him as the company grew.

At first, he began using materials that caused less harm to the environment, and he gave away 1% of sales each year. Eventually Patagonia became a certified B Corporation and a California Benefit Corporation, writing their values into their corporate charter so they would be preserved. In 2018, he changed the company's purpose to, "We're in business to save our home planet."

But Chouinard still didn't feel like they were doing enough to address the global environmental crisis. This would be the biggest mountain he ever climbed in his life. How would he help tackle this worldwide problem? How could he, one person, change the fate of the planet? He *alone* couldn't, but he could *with others and by making a commitment* to serve the environment.

There were no trail maps for this particular path, so they created their own. He could have simply sold Patagonia and donated the money, but he never could have guaranteed that the buyers would be the stewards he hoped they would be. Another would have been to take the company public. Again, he worried that with the pressure

---

* Yvon Chouinard, "Patagonia's Next Chapter: The Earth Is Now Our Shareholder," *Patagonia*, September 14, 2022, https://www.patagoniaworks.com/press/2022/9/14/patagonias-next-chapter-earth-is-now-our-only-shareholder.

† Chouinard, "Patagonia's Next Chapter."

to please shareholders, the company would have to compromise their principles and core mission. So, "instead of 'going public,' you could say we're 'going purpose,'" Yvon stated.*

*Going purpose.*

That is the Second Mountain. This is when your Plan To Take On the World is fully activated and you can achieve the impossible. For Yvon, the NBDB wasn't conquering another summit or growing Patagonia bigger—it was redefining what business itself could be. Everyone has their "something" they have never done before, the mountain they never climbed. And that is exactly where we are headed next.

*How can you get everything you didn't even know you wanted?*

---

ACTIVITY

## Finding Your Second Mountain

Pull out a piece of paper or journal and respond to any or all the questions that resonate with you right now:

- Review your career: Look at your first mountain. What was it? Is it your soul's calling *or* what "society" told you success is?
- What were you told or what did you believe success was? Where did you learn that story of success? How old were you? Who told you that story? Family, friends, TV, movies, books?
- Do you routinely set goals for yourself to achieve? Are these your own? Or what you see others doing and also feel compelled to do?
- Do you feel the need for outside validation from others? For example, are you waiting for a parent to tell you they are proud of you?

---

* Chouinard, "Patagonia's Next Chapter."

Do you feel you need to or should carry on the family craft, business, etc.? Have people consciously or unconsciously told you to?

Have you ever achieved something and woke up the next day feeling unfulfilled or disappointed? What was missing?

What have you done lately that made you feel satisfied or fulfilled? What were you doing? Who were you with? Can you articulate what that feeling was?

Part 3

# Share Your Plan with the World

Let's recap. You're now on your Hero's Journey. You've uncovered your origin story, chosen love over fear as your compass, and learned to differentiate passion from purpose. You've faced your Shadow Self, discovered your natural talents, stepped outside your comfort zone, and tapped into the wisdom of both mind and body.

You've also done real work—that's "love made visible." You've expanded your vision, learned how to face obstacles, and turned rejection into resilience. Maybe you've already taken a leap of faith. Maybe you've even tasted success. Which naturally leads to the next question: What now? How do you sustain greatness? How do you take your passion, your purpose, your life's work—your love—and share it with the world?

It's time to share your plan with the world.

In these closing chapters, we're going to move fast—but I don't want you to read fast. These aren't highlights—they're launchpads. Use them to reflect, to reset, to ask what this looks like for you. You'll hear about some of the most inspiring, generous, accountable, and vulnerable people who used their passion, purpose, and work to achieve more than they ever imagined.

Again, I'm not only advocating for chasing external goals (more money, more fame, more power) just for the sake of having *more.* It has been my experience and the experience of many PTTOW! members that money, fame, and influence came as a *result* of being generous, accountable, vulnerable, and working with others. It's a happy byproduct—not the goal, and not the definition of success.

My hope has always been that PTTOW! could be a community where members are *more because we come together to do great things.* This part will help you take a dream that once seemed impossible and share it with the world as your new reality.

# Chapter 16

## Go Further with Irrational Generosity

> This is what I find most magnetic about successful givers: they get to the top without cutting others down, finding ways of expanding the pie that benefit themselves and the people around them. Whereas success is zero-sum in a group of takers, in groups of givers, it may be true that the whole is greater than the sum of the parts.
>
> —Adam Grant, *Give and Take: Why Helping Others Drives Our Success*

Renowned author of several bestsellers and Wharton professor Adam Grant shared one of his most profound leadership concepts in his book *Give and Take: Why Helping Others Drives Our Success.* His research revealed he could group leaders into three distinct categories—or what he calls "givers, takers, and matchers."

According to Grant, "matchers" (transactional leaders or what I call "tit for tatters") operate principally on the basis of fairness—quid pro quo. They strive to balance helping others and advancing their own interests.

"Takers," on the other hand, are primarily concerned with their own success and advancement, and rarely prioritize the well-being of their team, organization, or customers/clients, let alone what is good for the world.

Last, there are what Grant calls "givers." These leaders focus on helping others and contributing to the success of their team or organization—and, by extension, the world. They are often the most effective leaders because they build strong relationships and foster a positive culture.* Grant argues that the best and most successful organizations thrive when they create an environment where givers can succeed.

When my cofounders and I began PTTOW!, we were committed to becoming an organization that operated differently than the status quo. We wanted our members to learn from each other and create projects and partnerships that have Never Been Done Before, while having a positive impact on the customers they served. Our goal was to be all about action. We believed that an idea was not good enough unless it could improve your business. We wanted to create a platform that spread positive and impactful messages to our members. Over the years, I have witnessed and been profoundly changed by the people we've invited into our community, summits, private forums, curated conversations, think tanks, and many more activities. In turn,

* Adam Grant, *Give and Take: Why Helping Others Drives Our Success* (Viking, 2013).

we have adopted what I like to think of as an irrationally generous approach to leadership.

We have evolved PTTOW! from the inside out and invited our members to create some of the most influential pillars and working groups to impact culture, such as the Gun Safety Alliance, originally conceived of by Kristin Lemkau, then the global chief marketing officer of JPMorgan Chase, to help reduce deaths due to gun violence. We launched the Social Justice Task Force, fighting systemic racism and empowering brands to make a meaningful difference in the age of Black Lives Matter. It is our action orientation that truly brings our community to life.

But, according to Grant, it's actually quite *rational* to be generous. The more you give, the more you receive. I am not the only one who thinks this way. I know my cofounders and fellow PTTOW! colleagues feel this way too. And most of our members share this philosophy.

One member that immediately comes to mind is Daniel Flynn, who cofounded the company Thankyou in Australia when he was a teenager. Flynn launched Thankyou in 2008 with Justine Flynn and Jarryd Burns. Its mission: to bridge the gap between extreme poverty and extreme consumerism by developing high-quality sustainable personal care and cleaning products and dedicate 100% of their profit to their mission. They were driven by an audacious, seemingly impossible question: *What if we could imagine a world where not one person lives in extreme poverty?* As a result, they formed the Thankyou Charitable Trust, whose vision is to see that question answered.

The trust commits all the money it receives (excluding bank and filing fees) to its impact partners serving vulnerable communities. But rather than requesting donations, hosting rubber-chicken dinners or fancy galas, or staging the various fundraising events that a lot of nonprofits create, they began to sell consumer products. Thankyou's goods aren't just any product—they have been voted the most sustainable brand of 2022 by Australian consumers. And they found creative ways to market their company on a budget, including viral consumer marketing campaigns like launching a pay-what-you-want book to raise money to help the organization expand. Thankyou's books, personal care and cleaning products, and baby care items all exist for their mission, and they give every cent (after paying all the costs involved in making great products) to the Thankyou Charitable Trust, which then distributes all of the money to their partners serving those living in extreme poverty. This is not a misprint.

Talk about irrational generosity!

Since they started, they have given away more than AU$18.5 million to change-making impact partners worldwide. How can a company survive by giving all of its profits away? According to Daniel, it's because they give away so much that they are so abundant and successful. He flips the usual logic on its head: The more they give, the more they grow.

I love this notion. At PTTOW!, members like Daniel Flynn are the exception rather than the rule. True, not all of our members give all of their profits to charity, but all of them believe in giving back in some capacity. Our membership includes solopreneurs, entrepreneurs, and Fortune 10 companies—and all show a commitment to improving others and the world. In fact, most of our members are working toward a profit, but all of them use a portion of their profit with the intention to do some good in the world. Thankyou, in particular, is fully committed.

Sebastian Terry introduced me to Daniel, and I was struck by his energy, pure soul, and generous spirit. He walks the walk. I invited him to speak at one of our events in 2017, and I can honestly say he had a profound impact on how I thought about our own company.

Up until I met him, I'll admit that as committed as I was to giving, I was equally consumed by the idea of our profit margin. What does the bottom line look like from an EBITDA perspective? After all, PTTOW! is a business; we have to pay employees and event spaces, not to mention keep the lights on. But Daniel got me thinking. His business was flourishing even though he had thrown all the traditional rules of business out the window. Then, when I heard his story and his mission, I was blown away.* He was hands-down the best business speaker I've ever heard. He had a way about him that was utterly captivating.

When he started Thankyou, major retailers weren't exactly rolling out the red carpet for him; not one would give him a meeting. So he decided to create a breakthrough stunt campaign, flying helicopters over two major supermarkets' head offices carrying banners with a message that thanked them for joining Thankyou in changing the world, if they chose to stock their product. Up until this point, both retailers had said no, but the stunt created a media sensation in Australia. After that, Thankyou became the bestselling hand wash at major retailers. The same retailers who said "no way" became the ones putting his products at the top of their shelves.

I am sure there were many people (including the retailers who eventually partnered with him) who thought he couldn't do it. Create a product that people would need and give all of his profits away?! Yet though his model defied business logic, his generosity has led Thankyou to become one of Australia's most successful small businesses/nonprofits. As Daniel says, "If you want to change the world,

* You can watch his main stage talk at https://www.youtube.com/watch?v=wlvgt4qyJZM.

you have to do something the world has never seen before." Or, as we say in PTTOW!, you have to be willing to do the NBDB.

Daniel's story reframes the question for every leader: What if impact isn't a cost—but a competitive edge? You don't have to give it all away as Thankyou does, but building purpose into your model might just be your greatest ROI.

Daniel isn't alone on the positive end of the generosity equation. Most of us have heard of Blake Mycoskie, founder of the shoe seller TOMS, which is world famous for their buy-one-give-one business model that many other companies have followed. Blake is also one of our Nelson Mandela Changemaker Award recipients, an honor we created in partnership with Kweku Mandela and his family to recognize leaders who embody President Mandela's legacy of justice, unity, and transformative change. Originally, we had hoped to honor the president himself with the PTTOW! Icon Award while he was still with us, but—true to his spirit of humility—he suggested, through his family, that we instead recognize modern-day activists carrying on his good work.

The award is given to visionaries who don't just succeed in business but also use their platforms to change lives and uplift communities worldwide. Blake earned that recognition for boldly reimagining what business can be. Since launching TOMS in 2006, the company has donated over 100 million pairs of shoes to people in need and continues to give away one-third of its profits to grassroots causes around the world.

For instance, TOMS partnered with ChildFund to provide new shoes to children in Liberia. Many families there struggle to afford school shoes, and children often share a single pair. This partnership has helped improve children's access to education and health. They also have partnered within El Salvador, Lithuania, and Tajikistan to distribute over a million pairs of shoes and winter boots to children in these countries. And shoes are just the tip of the iceberg; they also contribute to improving children's well-being through wellness, dietary, and educational services. They help out impoverished children here in the US too; for example, during Hurricane Harvey, TOMS partnered with Save the Children to advocate for emergency fundraising efforts.

From the smallest, entrepreneurial endeavor like Thankyou, to larger ones like TOMS, it's possible to be both audacious and successful. Even the massive companies we work with have made giving back the bedrock of how they operate. The fandom that TOMS and Thankyou have created has truly helped make their products and companies even more popular. Even the Fortune 100 companies we've invited to PTTOW! make giving a priority. I would venture to say that the reason these companies are successful—the secret sauce to their growth—is their commitment to giving. And if you don't believe me after these two examples, look no further than one of the most successful companies in the world—Procter & Gamble (P&G).

With brands like Tide, Dawn, Febreze, Swiffer, Pampers, Bounty, Charmin, Olay, and many more, P&G is massive. But they also have been committed to environmental and sustainability initiatives, as well as to giving back to their communities—and expanding the markets of minority communities. One of my favorite leaders is Marc Pritchard, P&G's chief brand officer, responsible for building the company's brand worldwide. He has been with P&G for over four decades and is dedicated to personally serving customers around the world . . . all while being what he calls a "force for growth and a force for good through community impact, equality and inclusion, and environmental sustainability."*

---

* "Marc Pritchard, Chief Brand Officer," Procter & Gamble, accessed March 13, 2026, https://us.pg.com/leadership-team/marc-pritchard/.

Katie Couric introduced me to Marc, who happened to be working on the same initiative as she: making media more inclusive. When many people in the world seem to be rolling back an interest in inclusivity, he and P&G began investing in and expanding in Black-, Hispanic-, and Asian-owned, operated, and targeted media markets to ensure brands were reaching all consumers in relevant and resonant ways. This didn't hurt them; by investing media in these markets, P&G has now reached even more customers. They have seen improved business in the last few years by driving growth for their brands and for their markets.

Many people have "limited" or "scarcity" thinking. They believe there are a finite number of pieces of pie, and if others get "some of the pie," there won't be anything left. Pritchard argues instead for abundant thinking: We need to make the pie bigger so everyone can partake. In fact, the pie is infinite, so everyone benefits when we expand it.

This step—being irrationally generous—is key to growth and expansion. You can't expect to receive what you aren't willing to give away. I am repeatedly blown away in my own life by how true this adage is. You must be willing to give to grow.

---

### ✴ ACTIVITY ✴

## Give to Grow

Take a moment to reflect. Answer these questions and be honest with yourself about your relationship with generosity.

- How do you define your relationship with generosity? When you give, do you also feel you receive?
- Do you tend to be a taker, a matcher, or a giver?

- In what ways could you contribute more—to your team, community, or relationships?
- What holds you back from giving more? What are you afraid might happen if you did?
- What's one thing you can do in the next week to practice generosity with no expectation of return?
- A week from now, reflect on what you did. How did it feel—and do you want to do more of it?

Chapter 17

# Become Radically Accountable

> Leaders must own everything in their world. There is no one else to blame.
>
> —Jocko Willink, former Navy SEAL, author of *Extreme Ownership*

Growing up on the ski slopes of Colorado, Molly Bloom had her sights set on Olympic gold, like her brother Jeremy, the two-time Olympian and ten-time World Cup gold medalist. But this isn't another skier-takes-gold success story. Molly never realized her ski-career hopes. They were dashed when she suffered a career-ending injury while attempting to qualify for the Olympics.

As the daughter of a clinical psychologist and ski instructor, this fate was by no means the story Molly had expected for herself. She'd had big goals, dreams, and ambitions—and suddenly found herself unmoored without a purpose. Now she was forced to pivot and find something different at the ripe old age of 22.

So, in 2002, she left the snowy slopes she had called home her entire life and set her eyes on a new horizon—sunny LA. Needing to make ends meet somehow, she started working as a cocktail waitress. It was there she discovered a new passion—poker. Her skill, acumen, and fearlessness caught the eye of her boss, and she was tapped to help run a high-stakes poker game at the famed Viper Room. It's not shocking that someone who once fearlessly stared down the fastest slopes in the world would also have the stomach for high-stakes poker. Her peers dubbed Molly the "Poker Princess" as she entertained celebrities, millionaires, billionaires, and titans of industry in the world's most expensive poker games. If there were an Olympic event for cultivating and pleasing clientele capable of building massive poker pots, she would have taken gold hands down.*

Then one day, it all came crashing down. Molly received a call from her office that said, "The FBI is here and looking for you." She knew she was caught. As she told us at PTTOW!, "I wanted to go home"—back to Colorado and her mom.

Indeed, her immediate response was to run away. She tried to book a flight back to Denver, but her credit card was declined. Then another was declined. And another. Finally, she checked her bank account balance, and lo and behold—her accounts had been frozen, and more than $9 million was gone—seized by federal authorities. Broke, out of work, and without a dime to her name, Molly had to face reality. Her life as she knew it was over. The high life, the celebrities, the money . . . all of it was gone. She had to start over again. She moved home with her mom and grandmother, and in her own words, "felt pretty sorry for myself." But she couldn't hide in her

* Robert Kolker, "Manhattan Fold 'Em," *New York*, June 28, 2013, https://nymag.com/news/features/gambling-ring-2013-7/index2.html.

mom's basement forever, so she started putting the pieces of herself together, and two years later she landed a job and moved back to Los Angeles. Five days after she moved into her modest studio apartment she was woken up by 17 FBI agents who, with guns blazing, handed her a sheet of paper—*U.S. v. Molly Bloom*, officially charging her with operating illegal poker games in New York.

Facing prison time and serious fines, Molly didn't know what to do. With her mother beside her, she flew back to New York to face her fate. Her mother helped her find a lawyer. Afraid, broke, and not knowing what to do, Molly asked her lawyer, "What's our strategy and what's our angle?" To this day I remember her repeating her lawyer's words to all of us at PTTOW!: "Our strategy and our angle is Integrity."

That was the game plan—Integrity. To tell the truth, to own her mistakes, make amends, ask for forgiveness, and move forward. In other words, she needed to be radically accountable.

Molly agreed with her lawyer. She said, "I was ready to return to integrity—no matter what the cost." And it wasn't cheap. The prosecutors offered her a cooperation deal; if she agreed, her money would be returned to her and she would be saved from prison. She decided to pass on the deal, and stand for her own mistakes.

That cost was a year of probation, 200 hours of community service, and between legal fees, fines, restitutions, and debts she wasn't allowed to collect, she was in the red millions of dollars. She pled guilty and was ready to move forward—not by fighting it, lying, or blaming, but by saying, "I want to be accountable." To be a better person. Someone who can be trusted. Someone whose word means something, who owns their mistakes, so they can be better. She paid her debt to society, wrote a book (that became the eponymous Oscar-nominated movie *Molly's Game*, written and directed by Aaron

Sorkin), and dedicated her life to telling her story and encouraging others to own their past. As Molly told us at PTTOW!, "Look at the things you've done and ask for forgiveness. After clearing out that wreckage from the past, you can move forward, in a way, to keep your finger on the pulse."

For me, integrity is the ultimate key to unlocking the next level inside you. Preserving integrity by walking the talk and being accountable for your actions takes courage, because to have integrity means you must be willing to own your choices—all of them. You can also own anything happening to you in your life and use it to your own advantage—*not to get ahead, but to get better.*

I like to say that there are two ways to go through life: Everything is happening *to* me, or everything is happening *for* me. When you go through life believing everything is happening *to* you, you are a victim of your circumstances who always finds someone or something to blame. But when you realize life is happening *for* you, you realize every event, every seeming mistake, misstep, lapse, experience, and change is happening so you can grow, learn, and become a better person.

Sure, you can say "there are no mistakes, only lessons," but part of being radically accountable is owning your part that you play in this life. Daily, we let people down. We say we'll be there on time, and we arrive 20 minutes late. We promise work will be done and don't deliver. We say one thing and do another. We're human. We all fail and mess up from time to time. The difference is how we respond to our mistakes, errors in judgments, or—in the radical case of Molly Bloom—illegal activities. Do we own them, correct them, and make a plan to move forward in a way that amends or atones for our behavior? Or do we avoid, deflect, or blame others for our mistakes, or just blame the world and call it bad luck? There is no bad luck or good luck. You make your own luck.

When you are on your way to taking on the world, understand that you will make mistakes, screw things up, and hurt people (even unintentionally). But will you have integrity? Will you make your own choices? Will you be able to "return to integrity—no matter what the cost"? The only way to prevent mistakes from happening in the future is to learn your lesson so you don't do it again.

Some of the greatest examples of owning their shit are the incomparable Navy SEALs. Over the years, we have invited the Navy SEALs to come and speak at our PTTOW! summits and run our breakout sessions. We've even had the elite SEAL Team 6 on the one-year anniversary of their raid that took down Osama bin Laden. Another time, a group of SEALs led a bite-sized (emphasis on *bite-sized*) version of their mind-blowingly intense training regimen. The purpose of the exercise was to encourage our PTTOW! members to step out of their comfort zones and understand what is truly required to operate on such an intense level—mainly integrity. If you can't be trusted, your team can't count on you. And if your team can't count on you, you are the weakest link, which literally could be life or death for everyone counting on you.

Mind you, the activity we had our members engage in wasn't life or death. But we wanted to introduce members to what it takes to operate on the highest quotient of both physical fortitude and mental acuity, while owning their shit and moving forward in the face of adversity.

I realize the Navy SEALs and Molly Bloom are extreme cases of integrity. Most of us will not have to face the US government in the court of law or flying unseen into Pakistan to capture or kill America's number-one enemy, but we all need to operate at a basic level of integrity if we want to succeed.

When I think of other great members of PTTOW! who operate in integrity, I think of Russell Dubner. When I met him 15 years ago, he was working at the strategic communications firm Edelman in New York. What struck me immediately about him was how amazing he was at building trust through communications. Today, he serves as the global chief communications officer at Boston Consulting Group (BCG), where he drives client-facing work in gaining trust as well as crafting key leadership principles.

When I met Russell, he was instrumental in shaping the Edelman Trust Barometer—an annual report published by Edelman that measures the state of trust in various institutions, including business, government, media, and NGOs. Russell has since created a company-specific set of analytics at BCG to measure and build stakeholder trust as part of the BCG Trust Index.

One thing he said to me that stuck out when he spoke to us all those years ago was, "Trust is earned when actions meet words." And that in a nutshell is what the Trust Index is. If you want to earn someone's trust, do what you say you're going to do—and keep doing it. This seems simple, but it's a lot harder than it looks. It means doing things when it's difficult, when it's uncomfortable—when, as in Molly Bloom's case, it gets in the way of your personal freedom. In the Navy SEALs' case, it means putting your life on the line. But whether you work for someone else or run a business, setting an annual goal on your review or leading a department, trust is foundational. If you want anyone to buy from you, believe you, or follow you, they need to trust you. And when do they trust you? When your actions reflect your words—in other words, when you display integrity. How you do small things is how you do big things. How you show up when no one is looking is how you show up for the world.

Trust and integrity—integrity and trust. If you want to go the distance, you will need both.

ACTIVITY

## Let's Get Real—and Start Taking Radical Accountability

A good way to recognize that you're not owning something is that you are blaming someone or something for where you are right now or who you are. Take a moment of reflection and think about what you aren't owning right now, then follow these steps.

### Step 1: Owning the Situation

- Reflect on a recent instance when you felt things didn't go your way or you were getting "screwed."
- Next, get to the root of where this story and situation began. Think of every step along the way, even when you said yes and were happy with this path and how things were going.
- Now, think of the moment things started going against you, getting out of your control, and not going your way. See how it was "all good" and even exciting, and everything you wanted, until it wasn't. Had you said yes the entire way, until it didn't suit where you wanted to go?
- Ask how can you take any accountability for the situation, by owning not just the good parts but also the bad ones. Instead of feeling pissed off, victimized, even enraged, can you see the role you had in getting to this moment?

### Step 2: Finding the Gifts and Silver Linings

- What, if any, are the hidden gifts or silver linings that came out of the situation?
- What lessons, if any, have you learned? What can you see happened *for* you, not *to* you?

# Chapter 18

## Radical Vulnerability

> Your life is like an egg. If an egg is broken by an outside force, life ends, but if an egg is broken by an inside force, life begins. And you have greatness inside of you, and what's inside of you is so much stronger than when it's on the outside.
>
> —Jim Kwik

In 2023, PTTOW! hosted our "Kintsugi" Summit, named after the Japanese art form of pouring gold into the cracks in broken pieces of pottery. It is also called "golden joinery" or "golden repair." Instead of disguising the cracks, or throwing something broken out altogether, those practicing the art of Kintsugi highlight and embrace the imperfections, thereby transforming or changing the piece into something more unique, more precious, more valuable and beautiful than before.

This practice also symbolizes a philosophy we can apply to our lives. Rather than hiding our flaws, imperfections, perceived failures, rejections, or heartbreaks, we should celebrate and appreciate these parts of our history. They make us stronger, more appealing—and even better people. As Rumi wrote, "The wound is the place where the Light enters you."

So many of us hide our imperfections, our weaknesses, our failures. We fear that if we show this side of ourselves, we will appear weaker—dare we say, more vulnerable. But what if I were to tell you that vulnerability is the special sauce, the main ingredient—even our superpower?

Earlier in the book, we talked about our origin stories. Often our story reveals our cracks, our broken pieces. But in overcoming them, we came back stronger, better, and more informed, enlightened, and prepared.

I and fellow members of PTTOW! believe the world of the future isn't going to be one of command and control. Rather, we believe firmly in heart-centered leadership. We have seen over and over again the failure of command-and-control ideology. Many leaders think that if they are "tough" and take "control," doling out orders without mercy or empathy, they will be more "respected" and powerful. Yet we know that thinking only the strongest, mightiest, and seemingly invulnerable will survive dooms us to failure. In the extreme, this belief does more than fail; it destroys, as every despotic leader from history has shown us. And it will always fail, because it's the weakest form of leadership.

The best and strongest leadership comes from the heart—from those who have the courage to reveal that they have a heart, that they feel, that they have experienced life's ups and downs, that they have survived and want the same for others.

When PTTOW! member Jim Kwik came to speak at our Kintsugi Summit, he spoke about how his superpower—his ability to speak, think, and write—came out of a vulnerable moment. In 1978, when he was just five years old in kindergarten, he ran to the window to see some firetrucks outside, sirens blaring. While attempting to climb up on a tiny chair for a better view, he fell into an iron grate radiator. Covered in blood, he was rushed to the emergency room. He was never the same afterward.

Before the accident, he had been creative, playful, curious, articulate. But suddenly he was shut down, reserved, with no ability to focus or remember. The injury had given him several processing issues, and teachers had to repeat themselves over and over.

One day, some children were teasing him, and a teacher came to his defense. Pointing at him, she said, "Leave that kid alone. That's the boy with the broken brain."

As Jim told our audience that day, "People can be very sincere, sincerely wrong." And that teacher was. He struggled with learning for the next 13 years. He worked harder than everyone for little results. He was often frustrated. But, with the help of his mother and father, he refused to let the words of others define and limit him, and ultimately he overcame his challenges.

Jim loved superheroes as a kid—and comic books saved him when conventional education couldn't. Comic books taught Jim how to read, but most importantly they also kept his dreams alive so that one day he, too, would find his inner superpower. And boy, did he. He poured gold into all the broken pieces. And after working on himself, he realized his brain was not broken; it just needed what he calls a "better owner's manual." Learning how to heal shattered Jim's own limiting beliefs—and over time, he pursued his passion to help others do the same.

For the past three decades, Jim has taught his learning techniques to students from institutions such as Harvard, CalTech, Singularity University, and the United Nations. He's also shared them with executives and employees from companies such as Google, Virgin, Nike, Zappos, GE, 20th Century Fox, Cleveland Clinic, and WordPress. For someone who had challenges with learning and public speaking, Jim now speaks and writes for a living—passing on what he has learned.

Jim Kwik is just one amazing example of how radical vulnerability works. Facing and embracing discomfort, uncertainty, and the potential for rejection or hurt requires real moral courage and exemplifies leadership. And it feels honest to people, because it is.

When I think of moral courage, leadership, and vulnerability, I also can't help but think of my friends Tariq and Carla Hassan, key leaders at McDonald's and JPMorgan Chase, respectively. They have openly shared the life-changing experience of fighting for their daughter Noor's life, after she was diagnosed with kidney cancer—a stage IV Wilms tumor—when very young. In 2012, four friends of the Hassans came together to form the Cycle for Survival to honor Noor's fight. The following year, the Hassans picked up the baton to create Noor's Army, which has raised money for Memorial Sloan Kettering's cancer research. Noor is now cancer free and thriving, has led the team for the past three years, and has raised $1.5 million. Together, by being so open about their own fight, they are changing others' futures.

Another reason you should try being vulnerable, besides healing, is that it cuts through the noise and small talk, creating a deeper connection right away. I've always been a fan of authenticity and honesty. It just feels better to me. The relationships I've built over the years that are the most real, engaging, and mutually beneficial are those that started from a place of vulnerability. Whether you're cultivating a friendship, partnership, romantic relationship, business, or leadership role, starting with vulnerability is always a good idea. If you do so for no other reason, remember this one: Your vibe attracts your tribe.

If you want to be surrounded by honest, authentic, heart-centered people who aren't afraid to admit their failures, mistakes, or broken parts, you have to be willing to do the same. I realize this might sound idealistic—even aspirational. It is. But it's not impossible.

Vulnerability is simply a methodology: By being true, you attract the truth. You save yourself and others a lot of time when you don't pretend to be something you're not. And you can't achieve great things—especially through partnership—if you can't be real first.

I remember a couple of years ago, I went to a Fit for Service (FFS) retreat in Austin, Texas, hosted by entrepreneur and author Aubrey Marcus. On the final day of the event, attendees were offered a chance to raise their hands, come up on stage in front of 150 fellow participants, and share a challenging experience. I raised my hand and Aubrey called me up.

I told the group—none of whom I had ever met—that during one of the weekend events, I barely had the courage to approach a fellow attendee I didn't know and ask her to join me in an activity. I was already out of my comfort zone, since I'd come to this retreat not knowing anyone, unlike the friendly bubble I usually inhabit in my own community. And I paid to go! Yet that wasn't the hardest part.

I shared how the exercise the day prior had flashed me back to being a shy 14-year-old who felt unseen by teachers. A time when boys and girls called me—a Russian newcomer—a commie, and when I was barely five feet tall entering high school. I shared that story with the group, and right after I spoke, the event ended.

I went back to my hotel without talking to anyone and had what Brené Brown calls a vulnerability hangover. I had to meditate and do breathwork for an hour just to manage my mind. I assumed the worst—that the group would think I was a fraud, an impostor, and that everything would fall apart. After all, why would PTTOW!

leaders follow Roman, who in high school might have been voted least likely to lead a community?

Yet when I went back to the final dinner and closing party that evening, I couldn't believe how many attendees came up to me to share how much my openness had helped them and reminded them of their own stories. My vulnerability hangover was gone, and I found I'd actually become more magnetic. I had one of my best evenings.

As the saying goes, "Your story owns you, until you finally own it." Only by being radically vulnerable did I finally gain power over my story. That's when I became more magnetic. One woman even told me she finally understood why I was the leader of the PTTOW! community: because I had shown strength and vulnerability by sharing my weakness rather than my accomplishments.

That's part of the Hero's Journey. My kryptonite became my superpower. The unseen kid had become the leader.

Since that retreat, I try and go first at events, sharing my vulnerabilities to help others feel safe and open up about their own challenges. That's how deeper connections form.

Another moment of radical vulnerability came from longtime PTTOW! member Ryan Detert, CEO of creator marketing platform Influential. When Ryan stepped onto the PTTOW! main stage, he didn't lead with accolades or company wins. He led with his heart.

He shared that he grew up without a father, and how that void was filled, in part, by a mentor named Clayton—his Big Brother through the Big Brothers Big Sisters of America program. Clayton wasn't just a mentor; he was family. He showed up consistently, shaped Ryan's worldview, and became the steady presence every kid deserves.

Years later, when Clayton was diagnosed with stage IV cancer, Ryan was there for him. Their bond had stood the test of time—and that love and loyalty came through when Ryan told his story. It wasn't polished or performative. It was raw, real, and brave.

By letting us into one of the most personal parts of his life, Ryan reminded us of something critical: Vulnerability isn't weakness. It's leadership. When we dare to be seen, especially in our pain, we create space for others to do the same. And that's where real connection—and healing—begins.

When Ryan shared his story, he wasn't just educating PTTOW! members on the power of Big Brothers Big Sisters—he was inspiring all of us to embrace our own vulnerability and, more importantly, to take action.

Someone who lives "being real"—authentic, open, vulnerable—and is an excellent leader because of it is PTTOW! member and friend Heather Malenshek, senior vice president and chief marketing officer for Land O'Lakes. Not long ago, she shared with members what she had been going through—something she had been keeping inside for a long time. Heather is married to a retired Navy veteran, and he recently had developed PTSD after losing several people from his squadron. His struggle became Heather's. It was a heavy and difficult time for their relationship, so they both began extensive therapy.

As a caregiver, she often worried about leaving him for long periods while she worked. She knew she was bringing that fear, worry, and anxiety to the office each day. So she had to get honest and real with her CEO, a heart-centered, compassionate leader who had set a great example. Heather felt strongly her team needed to know too.

"At the core of my leadership is authenticity," Heather told me. "I don't think I could be a good leader unless people really know who I am, and I know who they are. I spend a lot of my time really understanding and getting to know my team at a deeper level."

To lead with empathy, Heather believes she has to know who her team is—their struggles, their celebrations, the good and the bad. And to do that, she models openness by sharing her own life, including her husband's struggles and her own mental health.

To her delight, she discovered that when she was vulnerable, "I was giving them permission to do the same thing." And they did. People came out of the woodwork to share their struggles—with an alcoholic partner, a difficult child, depression, anxiety, and more.

When we asked Heather to speak to fellow members, unbeknownst to us, her husband was in a particularly serious struggle. She admits, "It was slightly terrifying for me to talk about this in front of a group of people I knew, but my therapist wisely pointed out that it would be an integral part of my healing to share in a safe environment. Speaking about my feelings and situation out loud actually took some of the power out of it, so that's what I did."

I can attest, as someone who was in the room that day, that we were all moved. As she stood on stage, we felt enormous love and compassion for her. I still do. And Heather was moved as well. She recently told me, "The wonderful thing about that moment is that I felt so much love and support in that room. There was no judgment. There was no pity. It was just a loving, supportive, compassionate environment. And my therapist was right. Speaking my truth out loud was a huge part of my healing journey. It was just an incredible experience to have in that room, at that time, with a group of people who were engaged, sending out so much love and support. I'm so glad I did it."

But before that moment, Heather hadn't always been so open. It takes time to feel comfortable enough to share, and she needed practice. She was raised to keep her work and personal lives separate—often pretending "everything is fine," as so many of us do at work. If something was going on at home, she stuffed it down. That isolation and loneliness weighed heavily. But once she began being more vulnerable, she felt less guilty about taking a day off or explaining an off day—and it helped others feel the same.

"So many companies talk about 'bringing your whole self to work.' But you can't do that unless you're honest about what's really going on," Heather says. "I feel that with the team, it creates loyalty. They know they have a safe environment where their feelings are supported."

Some might think this softer approach would lead to people taking advantage of her, but Heather has found the opposite. "I think it's just giving them the opportunity to bring their authentic selves to work. And because of that, I have an amazing team of people who are loving, compassionate, and supportive. I have people who will step up and say, 'If you need time off, I'll backfill you.' Or, 'I'm going to move things around so you have the time and space to take care of what you need to take care of.' To me, that is worth its weight in gold."

Heather wishes more leaders could create teams like this—and so do we at PTTOW! She also wishes she had learned this earlier in her career. She wants people to know they don't have to suffer alone. So now she makes it a practice to show up as her whole self at work and to check in on people. "Whether it's a text, an email, or a quick phone call—you never know when it might come at just the right time."

And that time is now. If you're thinking of someone—reach out. And if you need help, don't be afraid to ask for it. Radical vulnerability will forever change you—and the people with whom you share your story.

The best part about being a leader who is vulnerable is that you see the impact almost immediately. You quickly discover how to create a culture of openness, safety, trust, and connection when leaders—whether they're project leads, department heads, coaches, or CEOs—intentionally make a point of being consistently vulnerable.

✳ ACTIVITY ✳

## Radical Vulnerability

What does radical vulnerability mean to you? How does it differ from other forms of vulnerability?

Take a few moments and reflect on a recent moment when you felt truly vulnerable, especially in front of others. Or consider something in your life that has been weighing on you that you have an opportunity to share (in a safe space, of course).

What is it?

What emotions were you experiencing?

What did you learn about yourself from that moment?

Write about a time when you shared something deeply personal. How did others respond? How did it affect your relationship with them?

There's a saying that "the story owns you, until you own the story." When you are vulnerable, you begin to own the story. It becomes a superpower.

Describe a fear or insecurity that you haven't shared with anyone. What holds you back from sharing it? How might sharing it change your perspective?

In what areas of your life do you feel the most guarded? What steps can you take to begin opening up in these areas?

Think about a time when you felt truly seen and heard. What made that experience possible? How can you re-create that sense of connection in your daily life?

Does being more vulnerable offer an opportunity for you to connect more authentically? If so, consider giving it a shot and start small.

How can you make vulnerability a superpower?

Pro tip: It is possible to overshare and not "read the room," so you have to use your intuition on when it's appropriate to be vulnerable and when it may not. If you're in a room full of leaders, talk about what has been weighing on you as a leader (versus saying something from your personal life). If you're somewhere where everyone is sharing something deeply personal about a past trauma, now is not the time to bring up your work insecurities. Instead, see if there's something vulnerable about yourself you can truly offer in the moment that would be of service to the crowd you're in. In particular, consider where you can take ownership of what happened in your life, work, home, or friends, depending on where and when you are speaking. I always suggest that if you're nervous, share something small, so you don't get a vulnerability hangover.

## Chapter 19

# Go Together to Achieve Great Things

> Alone, we can do so little; together, we can do so much.
>
> —Helen Keller

Now is the part of your Plan To Take On the World where you really level up—and take things beyond your wildest imagination. How?

Relationships. People. Going together.

The old adage holds true: "If you want to go fast, go alone, but if you want to go far, go together." There are no singular heroes. Not even a single superhero can save the entire world—they need to work with others. Circling back to how we started with the origin stories of famous superheroes, I'd like us to consider *Avengers: Endgame*. After Thanos wiped out half the beings in the universe, several superheroes realized they needed to create a plan to save the world—a PTSTW!, if you will.

How did they do it?

They decided they needed to combine their forces and work together. And like every good organization, they broke out into teams to get the various jobs done. Iron Man, Captain America, Hulk, and Ant-Man made up one team. Thor and Rocket Raccoon were another. Nebula, War Machine, Black Widow, and Hawkeye were the final team. The only way they succeeded was by dividing and conquering through space and time and, most importantly, by combining all their superpowers (talents). And even in the end, they still needed even more backup—so (spoiler alert) Spider-Man, Black Panther, and the Guardians of the Galaxy joined in to ultimately help defeat the evil Thanos.

Now, we may not be superheroes who have to save the world (though I do think of us as modern-day superheroes), but our work can feel just as serious and our unique talents just as necessary. And we, too, need an army of superheroes who use their own powers, talents, purpose, and big hearts to come together to do great things. You can't be everything to everyone—you need to rely on each other's unique abilities and strengths if you want to take on the world.

When I traveled to India several years ago, a favorite PTTOW! member of mine joined: Nick Drake. Nick is now the VP of global marketing for Google, but back then he worked for T-Mobile. Spending time with him in a monastery with Tibetan monks, I realized he was as far from the corporate "marketer" type as you could possibly imagine. Clearly he was a man full of heart and empathy, and someone willing to listen to others and show up for them. Everything about him screamed authenticity. I have seen that heart at work as a PTTOW! member. He has used his abilities to partner with others to bring change—not just to the companies he works for, but also to the organizations he champions, like Team Rubicon, a PTTOW! family team.

Team Rubicon is a nonprofit that unites the skills and experiences of military veterans with first responders to rapidly deploy emergency response teams in communities struck by disasters. In 2018, T-Mobile announced the company was doubling its Home Runs for Hurricane Recovery (#HR4HR) donations during the MLB World Series. T-Mobile gave $10,000 for every home run to Team Rubicon, plus $2 every time anyone—T-Mobile customer or not—posted the #HR4HR hashtag to Twitter or Instagram. With the help of baseball fans everywhere, T-Mobile raised over $4 million for Team Rubicon. Several organizations cooperated to support those struggling from hurricane disasters—and it all started with relationships and an open-hearted willingness to help.

And that willingness to partner seems to be the key ingredient to success.

Take Andrea Perez. Currently serving on the board of directors for Hims and Hers after top brand and marketing positions at Nike for Brand Jordan and PlayStation, Andrea knows the power of partnership and bringing others along to do great things. In fact, when I think of Andrea, two words come to mind: audacious and brave. She's unafraid of going against the status quo. She believes deeply in teamwork—through her work at PlayStation, which is literally about gaming with teams, and at Nike, where collaboration is essential.

She is also an outspoken LGBTQ+ leader who champions inclusivity, especially for fellow Latinas. She walks the walk. She says, "This is who I am. Now take my hand, and let's start moving—together." And what I love about her is that she's a huge advocate for mentoring, especially young Latina women. She is adamant that they should be proud of who they are and who they represent, and she wants them to know that their unique experiences matter and they deserve a seat at the table.

For Andrea, partnerships aren't just between organizations (though those are great too). She believes in mentoring individuals—or, as she says, "bringing people up with you." Too often, in our race to the top or our desire to "take on the world," we see people as competition rather than partners who can help us all go further. Andrea has said, "For some of us it was a difficult ride to get where we are now, so let's make sure we pave the road and invite others in."* At Nike, she often set aside three hours a week to mentor those who sought advice about their careers.

One of the biggest lessons Andrea shares with her mentees came from her own mentor, Cristian Corsi, her general manager at Nike Mexico. He had a sign in his office that said, "The desk is the worst place from where to see the world." Andrea believes this wholeheartedly. It's helped her stay more open to what's happening away from her desk—with her team and on others, at organizations and industries, with consumers—and the world. Reaching out beyond the four walls of your office not only creates new partners and friends; it also makes you a better human. And we could all afford to be better at that. We could all be more inclusive and think about the world beyond our own experiences.

Someone who has helped me—and so many other people—rethink inclusiveness and opening oneself to the world outside is Mindy Scheier, a former fashion designer and the founder and CEO of Runway of Dreams and Gamut Management. She also spoke at our Kintsugi Summit. During her talk, she introduced me and our

---

* Vivian Nunez, "This Latina Nike VP on Why She Sets Aside Three Hours a Week to Mentor Others," *Forbes*, January 7, 2019, https://www.forbes.com/sites/viviannunez/2019/01/07/this-latina-nike-vp-on-why-she-sets-aside-three-hours-a-week-to-mentor-others/.

PTTOW! members to the world as people with disabilities experience it. She shared the challenges they face daily, and revealed that there are far more people with disabilities than most of us thought—in fact, they are the largest minority group on the planet. According to Mindy, one in four people lives with a disability. That means 1.8 billion people worldwide, with an estimated $13 trillion of spending power.

For Mindy, this is a personal calling to bring awareness and create change in consumer culture for people with disabilities. When her child struggled every day with tasks like buttoning shirts, putting on pants, or pulling them over his leg braces, she felt her heart break, powerless to help him.

Then one day, her son came home from school and said, "Mom, I want to wear jeans. I don't understand why everybody else gets to wear jeans, except for me." It was a gut punch. But she told our members that the moment reminded her how important clothing is to people. After all, clothing is how we express our identities and show up in the world. Most of us without disabilities take this for granted.

In that moment, Mindy found her purpose. It came in the form of a massive goal: changing the fashion industry to be more inclusive of people with disabilities. In 2014, she founded Runway of Dreams to raise awareness of the need for adaptive clothing. In the fashion industry, adaptive clothing is developed for people who have difficulty dressing themselves, including those with disabilities and older people.

In 2016, her company made fashion history when it partnered with Tommy Hilfiger to create the first mainstream adaptive-clothing line, now called Tommy Adaptive. That breakthrough opened the floodgates for other brands—Target, Zappos, JCPenney, LVMH, and even companies in other industries—to wake up to this consumer trend.

To support this flood of need, she created Gamut Management, the first consulting and talent management company exclusively representing people with disabilities. Gamut works with companies to help them navigate the adaptive space and become disability competent. For example, when Victoria's Secret realized they were missing a huge segment of their consumer base—women with disabilities—they turned to Gamut. VS didn't truly understand who this consumer was, so Gamut introduced them to women of different ages, disabilities, and ethnicities, ensuring that product teams learned directly from their experiences before designing.

Before working with Gamut, VS had already started prototyping without really understanding what these women needed, so they had to start again. Lesson learned: In true partnership, you must listen, learn, and then work together. Eventually, VS designers realized they could modify a bra so more consumers could wear the same product. By using magnets as a front closure instead of a hook-and-eye, they changed the bra game—not just for people with disabilities, but for everyone.

Many products in our world began as innovations for people with disabilities—or became transformative through accessibility. Closed captioning, for example, was created for the deaf and hard of hearing and is now used by millions every day. Voice-to-text and speech recognition were developed to assist those who couldn't type or speak and are now embedded in our daily lives. Eyeglasses were once a medical device; today they are both essential aids and a multibillion-dollar industry. The list goes on. The greatest innovations happen when we look with our hearts as Nick did, beyond our desks as Andrea did, and beyond ourselves to the world as Mindy did.

Through the years, we at PTTOW! have done this, too, and we've watched organization after organization, person after person, do the same. I think of all the seemingly unlikely combinations of organizations and people working together to make big things happen.

For example, Kory Marchisotto, president of e.l.f. Brands, partnered with Craig Brommers, chief marketing officer of American Eagle, to create a totally unexpected business concept and launch. The two culture-shaping super-brands—both favorites in the semiannual Piper Sandler Taking Stock with Teens survey—discovered that by combining forces, they could create more opportunities for people to express themselves through beauty, fashion, and more. By bringing their brands together, they reached new audiences, especially coveted Gen Zers.

e.l.f. Cosmetics created a limited collection to craft a "jean-ius" look: the Denim Daze Eyeshadow Palette featuring blendable blues, the dark-denim-to-perfect-pink Perfect pHit Lip Balm formula, and the Get Cheeky Clay Mask. They also launched a campaign called "From Selfie to Belfie." A selfie captures only a makeup look, but a belfie captures both the best jeans and makeup looks.

Content creators supported the campaign using a custom TikTok Community Filter and a song co-created by e.l.f. and American Eagle to set the vibe across TikTok and Spotify. With user-generated submissions in hand, the companies crowned a "Jean Queen" to complement the "Belfie Queen," actress Carlacia Grant.

All of this started with a conversation between two people who decided to go together rather than go alone. And they aren't the only companies doing this.

There's also Seth Klugherz, one of our founding members. Seth is a master of building cultural relevance for global brands, especially in his work with candymaker Haribo. Over the past few years, he's brought to life some of the most unexpected and talked-about collaborations in the industry: Haribo × Vans, Haribo × Cleveland Cavaliers × Jeff Hamilton (fashion designer and another longtime PTTOW! member), and most recently, Haribo × JENNIE of K-pop combo BLACKPINK—a global partnership brought to life in collaboration with fellow PTTOW! member Peter Szabo. These projects aren't just campaigns—they're what happens when bold vision meets the right room, the right people, and the right moment.

PTTOW! member Bea Perez, the executive vice president and global chief of communications, sustainability & strategic partnerships officer for Coca-Cola, oversees a diverse portfolio and manages networked teams that lead and support the company's business objectives.

Until January 2022, Perez oversaw Coca-Cola's strategic marketing assets, including renewal of the partnership with the International Olympic Committee, all global marketing, and the marketing activations for FIFA—which we at PTTOW! were proud to play a part in accelerating.

In 2017, with Perez's guidance, Coca-Cola partnered with soul and hip-hop powerhouse Aloe Blacc to create music for the company's global FIFA World Cup campaign—the largest campaign in Coca-Cola's history. The song, "The World Is Ours," was written specifically for the World Cup campaign brief by producing pair Rock Mafia and performed by David Correy and Aloe Blacc in the US. They created and produced 28 versions of the song, each targeted to specific markets worldwide.

Bea was, of course, responsible for the vision, the collaboration, and making it a reality. I love this story because I see so clearly the hand of PTTOW! in these bridges and connections that have formed during our gatherings—and in the friendships, partnerships, and conversations that continue long after the events are over.

And of course, none of it would be possible without the relationships I've formed over the years with trusted business colleagues and friends.

For example, my friend and PTTOW! member Lori Feldman, founder of Redefine Music Advisors and former chief marketing officer at THE.TEAM, has been a huge force behind bringing some of the world's most impactful music and sports talents to PTTOW!.

Over the years, Lori has introduced Michael Bublé, Andra Day, Scout Bassett, Diana Taurasi, Echosmith, Linkin Park, and many more to our members. These moments gave our community opportunities to explore partnerships, share passions and unique experiences, and enjoy once-in-a-lifetime performances.

I invite you to visit our website, pttow.com, and explore our Partnerships and Projects pages, where you'll find more than two hundred collaborations born out of PTTOW!: Janelle Monáe and Pepsi, Revolt and Target, Mastercard and ChangeUp, Cheesecake Factory and Bounteous, National Geographic and *Breaking2*, Discovery and GoPro and iHeartMedia, Paris Hilton and Dash Media, and so many more.

But beyond the big names and the marquee partnerships, what moves me most is what these moments represent: leaders choosing to step out of competition and into collaboration. That's where the magic happens—not just in the headlines, but in the trust, courage, and creativity it takes to build something that's never existed before.

When COVID hit, everything stopped. Overnight, events disappeared. For most people, that meant canceled concerts, meetings, and conferences. For us, it meant our entire identity was at stake. What are we without our gatherings? What am I, if I can't bring people together?

I'll be real with you—there was a night I found myself staring at the ceiling, wondering if this was it. Ten years of blood, sweat, and tears disappearing in a heartbeat. The community we had nurtured . . . gone. But then another thought cut through: *This is exactly when our members need us most.*

Their jobs didn't vanish. If anything, they grew heavier. They were leading teams through fear, layoffs, and uncharted decisions.

We had two options: Wait it out and likely fail—or step up. The choice was easy.

Resilience felt like the wrong strategy, like clawing back to where we'd been. We weren't trying to return to the past—we wanted to spring forward. What we needed was agility. Out of that mindset came Project Bear Hug.

At first, that meant Zoom check-ins: *Are you and your loved ones okay? What challenges are you dealing with today?* But reaching hundreds that way was impossible. So I recorded a personal video (with my cofounder Jim doing the filming in my dining room) for every single member—reminding them what they meant to us, asking if they were okay and how we could support them. We hosted our first-ever real-time virtual event (the first of several), one-on-one connections, peer-to-peer check-ins, and private forums—many of which felt like group therapy.

And here's the part I'll never forget: Our members showed up for us too. They called to check in. They asked how they could help keep the community alive, embraced our pivots, and together made the Bear Hug mutual.

One of the greatest lessons I learned during this crisis was that experimentation—even failure—was celebrated. Before COVID, we hesitated to launch untested ideas, afraid of letting down our Fortune 500 members. Suddenly, tearing up the rule book was what earned respect. As Clayton Christensen warns in *The Innovator's Dilemma*: Disrupt yourself, or an outsider will.

And then something unexpected happened. While so many event-driven organizations struggled, we grew. We attracted more C-suite leaders and their teams. The caliber of the community rose. Not because we had the perfect plan, but because we'd made a simple decision: to be present, to meet our members where they were, and to spring forward.

Looking back, I realize that community isn't proven when the lights are bright and the stage is big. It's proven in the dark nights, when everything feels like it's falling apart—and you decide to show up for each other. That's what it means to go together to achieve great things.

The spirit our community exhibited while carrying us through COVID was the same spirit that has borne us through the last 15 years of building PTTOW!. And when I think about that journey, I think first of the people who have walked alongside me as we built this together.

None of this would exist without my cofounder and brother-in-arms, Jim Sullos. From the very first spark of PTTOW! to every curveball we've missed, caught, built on, and turned into magic, he's been my creative partner and the trusted soul I've leaned on. His brilliance, calm presence, and relentless commitment to creative excellence have shaped this movement more than most will ever know. I am so grateful to have him walking beside me, believing in the impossible, and cocreating something that has touched so many lives. I'm also grateful to my cofounder Terry Hardy, whose spirit and early support gave me the confidence to begin this journey. Together, they've both played an integral role in bringing this vision to life.

Of course, there's also the team itself at PTTOW!. From the very beginning, I've been surrounded by partners, teammates, and right-hand leaders who have helped carry this vision forward. I'm deeply grateful for Ryan Boughan, our president and chief operating officer, whose strength, clarity, and vision continue to guide our community with both steadiness and heart. His leadership has been pivotal in steering PTTOW! forward, ensuring that our mission not only endures but grows stronger year after year. And much of the epicenter of what comes to life within PTTOW! flows through programming and talent, which Samantha Rabstein has masterfully led. As our chief product and communications officer, she has been instrumental in cultivating the ideas that shape our culture and in working closely with the extraordinary talents who bring them to life. I could not have written this book without her. Her expertise, word wizardry, innovative thinking, positivity, superb editing, and audaciousness have fueled me and pushed this project further.

Kathlene Stakely is the driving force behind our events and operations, bringing precision and purpose to everything she does. Her unwavering and decisive leadership, paired with her consistency, creativity, and commitment, has been the backbone of countless unforgettable moments that define the PTTOW! experience. Our membership team—Ryan Brenner, Nicole Rosofsky, and Leann (Scibelli) Capraro—are the architects of connection, pouring themselves into nurturing relationships and weaving together the fabric of our community. Their fingerprints are on every bond created, every sense of belonging felt, and every spark that keeps PTTOW! thriving. Together, we can go so much further than we could ever go alone.

And beyond these leaders, there is the rest of our PTTOW! team—an extraordinary #DreamTeam without whom none of this would be possible. They are the heartbeat of our organization, pouring their talent, dedication, and creativity into every detail that makes our community what it is. My role is to empower them and create the space for each one to bring their full selves to their work, unlocking their greatest potential along the way.

Everything I do, I do better when I am surrounded by—and held accountable to—my team members. We couldn't possibly create experiences that captivate, wow, and awe without the individual contributions of everyone around me.

✷ ACTIVITY ✷

## Going Together

Are you a lone wolf or a team player?

When you think of a current project, think of who can be an unlikely partner or collaborator, as those often end up as the best ones.

What do you have in common? Similar customer?

What are your differences? Different products?

How can 1 + 1 = 3? Think of artist collaborations as cross-overs, like Avicii + Aloe Blacc from "Wake Me Up" (a #1 song).

Who in your network shares a similar passion or goal, and how can you reach out to them for support or collaboration?

What unique skills or resources do you possess that could benefit others working toward a similar objective?

How can building a community around your goal or dream enhance your motivation and drive?

What experiences have shown you the value of collaboration, and how can you apply those lessons to your current pursuits?

What specific steps can you take to create meaningful connections with others who can help you achieve your goal or dream?

Chapter 20

# Create Experiences That Captivate, Wow, and Awe

> To move the world, we must first move ourselves.
>
> —Socrates

As someone who stands on a stage and welcomes speakers, I have had a unique vantage point for watching a crowd react. I can see when the crowd is enraptured, stunned, eager to learn more, captivated, moved to tears, or in awe. Sometimes I see all of these emotions while one person speaks. These occasions happen more often than you might imagine at PTTOW!. But one moment stands out—in 2017, Claire Wineland shared her story with us.

Born with cystic fibrosis, a progressive and terminal genetic disease, Claire had never known a "healthy" day in her life. Most people diagnosed at birth do not live to see their 25th birthday—and Claire spoke to us when she was 20. She had spent a quarter of her life in the hospital, endured more than 35 surgeries, and was taking more than

50 medications daily just to survive. Standing before us, she wore a backpack that carried her portable oxygen. Other than the tubes running to her nose, no one would have guessed Claire was nearing death. She was so full of life, enthusiasm, and wisdom.

She said, "I'm not here to give you an inspirational talk. I'm not here to teach you guys how to fix yourselves, how to fix your problems, how to get over your challenges. I'm here to show you that there's a way to take your entire experience as a human being—all of the beautiful and the painful and the joyous and the suffering—and make something from that. Not run away from it, not shy away from it, but make something from it."

The theme of our summit that year was "Losing Sight of the Shore." Claire wisely pointed out that water represents chaos. You can build an entire city that can be crumbled by one wave. And yet, all of life—all the infinite possibilities, wonder, and amazement of being human—came from water, from chaos, from a giant melting pot billions of years ago. When you lose sight of the shore, you're literally jumping into that chaos, into that messiness—LIFE—and then you're forced to make something from it.

Sometimes the best people to teach us about life are those who know the precious value of it, who understand that every moment, even the painful ones, matter. Claire nearly died when she turned 15. Losing oxygen, unable to breathe, she slipped into a coma. Before she did, she remembered feeling a deep grief, as if she were losing a friend—and that friend was herself, the life she wouldn't get to live. She realized in that moment that it doesn't matter how much you prepare yourself for death—when it happens, you grieve the life you had and all the possibility that lay before you.

As doctors began to intubate her, Claire told us, she thought, "I never, ever want to be healthy. If I make it out of this, I don't want to be cured. Because I looked around at every single healthy person in my life—every single person had exactly what they felt they wanted—and yet we were in the same boat. We were two people just trying to make something of our lives. And it made no difference to me whether I was healthy or whether I was sick. I had something I needed to do in the world."

She woke up three weeks later, defying the doctors who had given her less than a 1% chance of survival. And she came back with what she described as "a fire under her ass."

Determined to make life better for herself and others in communities where children were dying, she stopped wishing for health and started living in the messy chaos of her reality. She and her mother founded a nonprofit to help kids like her—and their families—do the same.

There was no support structure for families of sick children. Claire's mother had lost her job caring for her, as do many parents facing the same circumstances. They had to spend so much time in the hospital that they often couldn't afford to keep regular work. So they created Claire's Place Foundation to help families cover bills, car payments, rent, mortgages, travel, and other expenses—so they didn't have to make the impossible choice between earning a living or sitting beside their dying child.

Claire knew she was never going to rid life of suffering. As she told our members:

> You're never going to run away from your pain. You're never going to run away from what it feels like to be human. Because being human is messy. It's messy and it's crazy and it's chaotic. It's like the ocean, and all you can do is dive in. If I've learned anything from living and dying and from being sick, it is that we all have something really incredible to share. We should stop trying to get over our problems, trying to get

rid of our problems, trying to jump through hoops to evade our problems. We should start using them, because they're one of the biggest gifts you will get.

When Claire finished speaking, she was almost out of breath—and so was the crowd. They were both speechless and breathless. In awe and shock, they jumped to their feet and gave her a standing ovation.

Just one year later, all of our hearts broke at PTTOW! when we heard the devastating news that Claire had died—from a blood clot, one week after receiving a double lung transplant. Her foundation still exists, and her wise words live on in the hearts and minds of all the people who have heard her story or read it in her book, *Every Breath I Take: Surviving and Thriving with Cystic Fibrosis.* I know I will never be the same after hearing her story. That is the power of words—of capturing hearts and minds.

Another leader who has studied the power of capturing hearts and minds is my friend and PTTOW! member Joe Marchese, cofounder and executive chairman of Human Ventures, a leading start-up studio and venture fund, and partner/cofounder of Casa Komos Brands Group, a portfolio of elevated hospitality brands. Before this, Joe served as president of advertising revenue for Fox Networks Group, where he oversaw multibillion-dollar advertising sales, research, and innovation for FOX Broadcast, FOX Sports, FS1, FX, FXX, and National Geographic. In other words, Joe knows what it really takes to captivate an audience.

When he came to speak to us, he argued (his word) that the single most valuable resource on the planet is attention. He believes the market for attention is broken—and it's affecting our personal, professional, and political lives. Divisiveness, extremism, terrorism, radicalism—all are fueled by this broken market. And if we don't fix it, it will only get worse.

"Once you give something or someone your attention, you can't take it back," he said, "because attention is equal to time. There are 24 hours in a day. We can't make any more of it. We make a decision about what we're going to pay attention to in every moment, but in the blink of an eye, attention disappears."

So the question becomes: Is what you're doing to get attention working? Does it create an emotion or a memory? "Because if it did," as Joe points out, "for the rest of your life, it'll shape what you do."

Just as Claire's story affected me and my fellow PTTOW! members, what we say and do has the power to affect others as well.

Attention, after all, is a precious resource. Joe reminds us that it's hard to capture and sustain another's attention, but when we do—or when someone captures ours—it shapes who we become, what we believe, who we love, and who we don't.

Joe says that knowing this forces us to ask, what are we going to do with our attention? Who will we spend it on? What will we do with the attention given to us? What impression do we want to leave with people? How are we gathering attention for our businesses? What are we doing in the battle for attention happening all around us? Better yet, how can we be part of making it better?

I like to think that what we do at PTTOW! makes this process better. It has been my life's purpose to create experiences that captivate, wow, and awe. I have immense gratitude for the community we've cocreated with our members. We scour the world to introduce people who have something incredible to share—people who walk the talk every day and use the attention they receive to make the world better.

Whether it's Kristin Lemkau or Katie Couric raising awareness about gun violence, or the Social Justice Task Force we created to confront issues facing BIPOC and LGBTQ+ communities, one of the keys to creating these experiences is being wildly creative.

PTTOW! member Jon Halvorson, now chief marketing officer of Kenvue, previously led global media, data, and digital strategy at Mondelēz International across brands like Oreo, Cadbury, Milka, and Trident. But he believes it's not just attention that's the world's most precious resource—it's creativity.

Jon points out that creativity can take a brand from low single-digit growth to 20% annual growth. Creativity brings opportunities, opens doors, and sparks conversations. He believes one big, bold idea can make an even more lasting impression.

I can't think of anyone better at running with a big idea than my friends and PTTOW! members Paris Hilton and Mark Weinstein, CMO at Hilton. Mark's team is responsible for Hilton's global network partners—American Express, Live Nation, The GRAMMYs, McLaren Racing—as well as a global portfolio of cobranded credit cards. One of his boldest partnerships was enlisting Paris Hilton, the great-granddaughter of the hotel chain's founder.

The "For the Stay" campaign pivoted from the idea that people travel for a destination to the idea that they travel "for the stay"—for the experience of the hotel itself. No one else was capitalizing on this idea, though we all know a hotel can make or break a trip. Who better to illustrate this than Paris Hilton, who doesn't leave home without her pets and designer luggage in tow? Talk about making a lasting impression and introducing Hilton to a new generation of travelers.

Partnerships, creativity, humor, shock, and thinking beyond what others are doing are key to capturing and keeping attention—and keeping you top of mind.

Raja Rajamannar, chief marketing and communications officer for Mastercard, has transformed it into one of the most iconic and recognized brands in the world. Using creativity, innovation, and multi-sensory marketing, he has extended Mastercard's reach by embracing

AI, Web3, inclusive design, and experiential branding. Under his leadership, Mastercard has been named by Amp Sound Branding the #1 audio brand for five consecutive years.* His work has been studied at Yale and Harvard, and he is the bestselling author of *Quantum Marketing: Mastering the New Marketing Mindset for Tomorrow's Consumers.* He also hosts his own Bloomberg TV show.

When Raja came to PTTOW!, he spoke about the evolving field of marketing and the importance of leveraging sensory experiences to build brand identity. He described how Mastercard developed its "sonic architecture" to create a consistent audio brand presence—the sound you hear when you use your card. You know it when you hear it. He also explained why Mastercard now uses only its symbol—not its name—on cards. The brand is universal, inclusive, and recognizable around the world.

The key to captivating an audience—what Claire and all the PTTOW! members taught me—was not just capturing attention or being creative and inclusive. At the core of it all is one word: heart.

Claire and our speakers showed us their deep, heart-centered purpose. They were vulnerable, fearless, unafraid to share their vision for the world. They were willing to do what they felt called to do. They faced insurmountable obstacles and incredible suffering, yet they persisted. They named their impossible goals, took their leaps of faith, and worked with others to take their vision further than they ever imagined possible.

And that has made all the difference. To me. To my team. To PTTOW! members. And now, I hope, to the world that has read this book.

---

* Amp, "Best Audio Brands," accessed March 14, 2026, https://ampsoundbranding.com/best-audio-brands.

PTTOW! is no longer the scrappy upstart fighting for its place—it's a cultural force with deep roots and global reach. But with that success comes a new challenge: no longer proving we belong, but remaining on the bleeding edge of culture. The first 15 years were about showing what was possible. Yet PTTOW! was never meant to be a company—it began as a passion project, a spark of curiosity and connection that grew into a business and movement.

In the beginning, it felt like launching a rocket ship. The hardest inch was just getting off the ground—convincing people to believe in something that didn't exist yet. That first inch took everything we had. But we did it. We broke through the atmosphere. Now we're in orbit. What comes next will require a different kind of propulsion—one fueled by imagination, creativity, and the courage to explore new frontiers.

That's the thrilling part. Neither the journey nor our world is slowing down—in fact, both are accelerating. The lessons in this book aren't an ending; they're a compass. They've carried me through obstacles, rejections, pivots, and leaps of faith. But just because I've lived this journey doesn't mean I have all the answers. I carry as many questions as before—only different ones.

Now that we've become part of the establishment, the questions are harder and the stakes are higher. At our best, PTTOW! helps leaders confront their toughest challenges and imagine what comes next. We create connections that unlock action. And we remind each other that the future isn't something to brace against—it's something we get to shape together.

PTTOW! began as a leap of faith. Today, it's proof of what's possible when vision meets community. And tomorrow? The story is still unwritten—but it's ours to write, and if we write it together, it can be nothing short of beautiful.

✷ ACTIVITY ✷

## Creating Experiences That Captivate, Wow, and Awe

What I love about Claire is that she didn't shy away from chaos. She dove right into it. She embraced her life and turned it into art—a beautiful story that left people breathless. I want you to spend a few minutes reflecting on these questions:

- What moments in your life have you felt alive and in awe?
- How do you typically respond to moments of wonder? Do you stop and take notice? What does it feel like in your body?
- Have you ever witnessed a moment so powerful it took your breath away? What made it unforgettable? The story? The delivery? The vulnerability and rawness? How could you repeat that in your own life?
- What would you regret or grieve if you didn't get to do it? Why aren't you doing it? What is stopping you?

# CONCLUSION

> The best journeys answer questions that in the beginning you didn't even think to ask.
>
> —Jeff Johnson

My favorite poet happens to be my friend IN-Q. He has said, "Whenever I feel lost, I know I'm going the right way. I am the journey that I'm getting to." He says it best in this poem:

*Everywhere you are*
*Is where you're supposed to be*
*So hopefully you're hopelessly*
*As lost as me*
*Because if you're not*
*you oughtta be*
—IN-Q

You are exactly where you are supposed to be. I am so grateful that you took the time to take my hand and go on this journey with me. I never promised to take you to a specific destination—because there is none.

Plot twist: You are the journey.

Your origin story is completely your own. You just have to understand it.

Your Shadow Work led you to embrace the parts of you that you spent years trying to hide.

You let love, not fear, be your guide.

You fanned the flames of your passion and helped it fuel your purpose.

You nurtured your natural talents.

You moved out of your comfort zone and routines and tried something new.

You learned how to tap into your body and feelings. Rather than being led by them, you learned how to become the rider and get control of your thoughts.

You went O.H.F.—became obsessed, put in the hours, and became completely focused.

You named your impossible goals.

You did the work—and realized work wasn't something you had to do, it was a labor of love—then realized that work aligned with your purpose is love.

You expanded your vision and dreams to go beyond possible to impossible.

You learned how to face and conquer obstacles, to master rejection and failure.

And when the time came, you took the leap of faith and went after the NBDB.

You got to the top of the mountain and achieved your dreams and realized there is so much more—life is not a singular mountain. You learned to redefine success and achievement.

You knew you had to share your story with others.

You became irrationally generous.

You became radically accountable and vulnerable.

You knew you couldn't go alone and saw how much greater we are when we work together.

You have this one life, and you get to make the journey anything you want it to be. You get to pick the people you want to take along for the ride. I for one am so grateful to have my crew, my friends, and family who have chosen to take this path with me. I have been made better by the process, and my hope is that you have too.

If I have done my job right, you feel inspired to take on the world—your world. You're ready to explore it, see it all, and ask questions you never thought to ask when you first stepped foot off the shore.

My journey is underway, and I am now and forever incredibly grateful (and in awe) of all the parts of it—the heartbreaks and the successes. I have all that I have today because of all the experiences that brought me here to this moment.

Now, it's time to step out on yours.

Five, four, three, two, one . . . PTTOW!

# NOW IT'S TIME FOR YOU TO CREATE YOUR PLAN.

With Roman's guidance and the support of the PTTOW! community, you'll be ready to take on the world.

Visit **RomanTsunder.com** for:

-Success Stories
-Videos + Podcasts
-Community + Events
-Additional Resources

and start to make your impact!

RomanTsunder.com

# GO BEYOND THE BOOK

Let Roman take you behind the scenes with exclusive PTTOW! videos, interviews, photos, and more, including:

Paris Hilton
Bert Jacobs
Quincy Jones
Van Jones
His Holiness Dalai Lama
Blake Mycoskie
Diana Nyad
Bob Pittman
Shaun White
Claire Wineland

alongside other moments featured in this book.

Visit RomanTsunder.com/bookbts

# ACKNOWLEDGMENTS

This book wouldn't exist without the people who truly helped shape it.

To my family—I love you. You are my foundation and my constant reminder of what actually matters.

To my mom, Lia Kushnir, whose strength, love, and resilience shaped who I am.

To my partner, Teresa—your constant love, patience, and wisdom have grounded me more times than I can count. You always offer perspective, honest advice, and clarity I don't always have on my own.

To my stepdad, Yasha Goldenberg, for your steady presence and support.

To my sister, Renee, and my nephew Nathan—you bring so much joy into my life. You are my biggest cheerleaders, unwavering supporters, and die-hard fans.

To my aunt and uncle, Alla and Vladimir Berelson—thank you for always showing up and being a constant source of support over the years.

To my cousins Roshelle, Dima, and Ilya—thank you for always being in my corner and for the support I know I can count on.

And of course, to our fearless leader, Yogi—who reminds us every day to lead with joy, loyalty, and heart.

None of this would be possible without the PTTOW! team beside me—I'm truly grateful for everything you do and the way you bring our vision to life.

To the mentors, advisors, and friends who have challenged me, supported me, and believed in this vision—you didn't just help shape this book, you helped shape how I think, how I build, and how I show up in the world.

I am especially grateful to our Advisory Board—Mark Stagen, Chris Robichaud, Alex Martinez, and Katharina McCarthy-Pesch—whose counsel has been a true lifeline.

Mark has been more than an advisor; he's a lifelong friend, mentor, coach, and confidant whose wisdom I return to again and again.

Chris began as a member and became a trusted guide—our sounding board, idea generator, and even at times the team's therapist—always showing up with perspective and heart.

Alex, a partner from across the pond, has brought clarity and strategic insight that have strengthened both me and PTTOW! as we pursue our north star.

And Katharina, through her care, thoughtfulness, and steady encouragement, has fueled our engine and reminded us of the values that keep us moving forward with focus and heart.

This book was built through real collaboration. Thank you to Mary Curran-Hackett for helping bring clarity and structure to ideas I've been carrying for a long time.

And to the PTTOW! community—past, present, and future:

You are the heart of this book.

This book is yours as much as it is mine.

What started as a passion project became something far bigger because of the way you show up—with curiosity, courage, and a willingness to build something meaningful together. The conversations, the vulnerability, and the action have shaped every page of this book and continue to shape my life.

This has never been about one person.

It's about all of us—connecting, creating, and building the beautiful world of tomorrow.

To everyone who has been part of this journey, in ways seen and unseen:

Thank you for being part of it.

# ABOUT THE AUTHOR

Photo by Magda Gamreklidze

**Roman Tsunder** is an entrepreneur, cultural architect, and co-founder of PTTOW! (Plan To Take On the World!), one of the world's most influential invite-only communities, known for bringing together leaders, founders, creators, artists, athletes, and changemakers to challenge convention and shape what's next in business and culture.

For nearly 20 years, Roman has convened transformative conversations and experiences featuring icons such as His Holiness the Dalai Lama, Quincy Jones, Halle Berry, Ryan Reynolds, and Paris Hilton, alongside leaders from companies including Google, Coca-Cola, Mastercard, Instagram, LVMH, and Netflix.

Born in Odessa, Ukraine, Roman came to America as a five-year-old refugee and developed a deep fascination with human connection, creativity, and what makes people come alive.

Inspiring social impact has long been at the forefront of Roman's career. He was a founding member of ALDER and co-founded

Movements.org, which brought together leading youth movement activists to empower young people to mobilize against violence and oppression.

A professional dreamer with a piercing vision for the future of culture, Roman has since founded, scaled, and invested in numerous start-ups and creative projects.

Today, Roman is known for helping leaders and organizations rethink what's possible—blending business, culture, storytelling, and purpose into experiences designed to create lasting transformation and growth.

Plan To Take On the World! is the culmination of those lessons, conversations, failures, breakthroughs, and impossible dreams.

He currently resides in Miami, FL and Los Angeles, CA.